How to Win Customers in the Digital World

in the Digital World

Total Action or Fatal Inaction

Springer
Berlin
Heidelberg
New York
Barcelona
Hong Kong
London
Milan
Paris
Singapore
Tokyo

Peter Vervest and Al Dunn

With Contributions by
Martijn Hoogeweegen, Nancy Foy Cameron
and Thomas Weesing

How to Win Customers in the Digital World

Total Action or Fatal Inaction

making every activity
– customer activity –
through complete communication

 Springer

Prof. Dr. Peter Vervest
Multimedia Skills
J. van Oldenbarneveltlaan 34–36
3818 HB Amersfoort
The Netherlands
and
Erasmus University Rotterdam,
Rotterdam School of Management
peter.vervest@totalaction.nl

Al Dunn
Multimedia Skills
Northfield
17 Berks Hill
Chorleywood WD3 5AG Herts
United Kingdom
al.dunn@totalaction.nl

with 34 Figures

ISBN 3-540-66575-7 Springer-Verlag Berlin Heidelberg New York

Library of Congress Cataloging-in-Publication Data
Die Deutsche Bibliothek - CIP-Einheitsaufnahme
Vervest, Peter: How to win customers in the digital world: total action or fatal inaction /
Peter Vervest and Al Dunn. With contributions by Martijn Hoogeweegen ... - Berlin;
Heidelberg; New York; Barcelona; Hong Kong; London; Milan; Paris; Singapore; Tokyo:
Springer, 2000
   ISBN 3-540-66575-7

© Springer-Verlag Berlin · Heidelberg 2000
Printed in Germany

Hardcover-Design: Erich Kirchner, Heidelberg
The image on the cover is based on the original idea of Brenda Renssen.

SPIN 10746747   42/2202-5 4 3 2 1 0 – Printed on acid-free paper

Foreword

Every organisation must strive for Total Action. Winning the customer in today's highly competitive and demanding world is the key to ensuring success. All managers and employees profess to understand this yet they find it incredibly difficult to perform together to achieve this. The 'digital world' is changing the traditional logic of business – we must now act fast and effectively to capture and retain increasingly demanding and sophisticated customers, be they individuals or organisations. Most customers demand much more than many organisations are able to deliver.

It is said that the inventor of the telephone believed its main use would be to let someone know that a telegram was arriving. Today we know there is a lot more you can do with a telephone... and all the surrounding digital business technologies. But you must be prepared to re-think why you are doing things the way you are. And why you are doing them at all. This is the starting point for 'How to win customers in the digital world – Total Action or Fatal Inaction'.

The authors confront traditional ways of organising with the capabilities of the new, digital business technologies. They are critical of the frozen behaviour of today's large organisations. They go back to the fundamental goal that business is about making money by satisfying customers. Digital business technologies enable entirely new ways of organising for the customer: But to benefit you must make the customer the point of decision making and truly organise from the customer inwards.

Like many business leaders, I have learned from experience that moving an organisation from its comfortable behaviour of the past to become the winning, customer-centric and high performance organisation needed for success today, is a major – some say almost impossible – task. Total Action approaches this issue by bringing together management thinking and experience in a new – perhaps unique – combination which ensures the necessary deep understanding of how to build an organisation with total performance for the customer and for its stakeholders.

It is not easy. Business is about making choices, about trade-offs. By using digital business technologies – be it simple e-mail or sophisticated web-based knowledge systems and electronic commerce – these trade-offs become highly visible. As we share the same information instantly, we can make better choices, choices which serve the customer and can be understood and acted upon by everyone within the organisation.

You may ask: Is this a realistic goal? But do we really have a choice? Let us recall the early days of 'total quality', the idea that quality is a responsibility of the total management, not just the quality department. Total Action, in this book, denotes the idea that customer satisfaction is the responsibility of the complete organisation, not just the sales or customer service departments. I find this a powerful idea. The authors make perfectly clear how digital business technologies help you to know about and understand individual customers; and how this understanding can and must be shared. This sharing of customer intelligence forms the basis of the new customer relationship, which in the digital world will be more important than ever.

I believe this book brings simple, powerful ideas on how to organise for customer success. It puts a manager's perspective into the amazing, but sometimes confusing developments, of today's telecommunications and computer technologies.

Ben Verwaayen
Executive Vice President and Chief Operating Officer
Lucent Technologies

Acknowledgements

Total Action results from our experiences with client organisations and our colleagues over many years. We acknowledge and apologise to our teams of consultants in Multimedia Skills. We acknowledge them for translating and developing our concepts and beliefs into business and for providing us with new insights and experiences. We apologise to them for patiently waiting for this book to be completed. Specifically we acknowledge Martijn Hoogeweegen of Multimedia Skills who, with his PhD. thesis on 'Modular Network Design', not only gave us a clear description of his research but was also active in ensuring the production of this final text. In addition, Miss Karen Verhoef, our assistant, must be acknowledged for her organising capabilities, patience and dedication. Thomas Weesing must be thanked for his stimulating ideas at the incept of this book.

Above all we acknowledge our clients. In particular those individuals who believed strongly enough in our concepts and experiences to introduce Total Action into their organisations when, often, they were surrounded by cynicism and disbelief. Let us not forget the customers of our clients who have had a major role in ensuring that Total Action works.

A major milestone in developing our concepts of Total Action has been a study trip to the USA during June 1998. We invited a number of people – whom we believed to be creative as well as critical of our ideas – to join us on a intensive study trip, meeting important USA business leaders, academics and entrepreneurs. They reviewed the first draft of this book – not always to the amusement of the authors. We would like to thank all participants for a most enjoyable and stimulating trip: mrs. Rinette Julicher (Dutch Ministery of Agriculture), Cees Ottevanger (Police Rotterdam), Freddy de Slachmuylder (PTT Post, nowadays TPG), Gert van der Weide (IBM), Vincent Everts (Mediaplaza), prof. Hans Wissema, Hakån West (Nokia), prof. René Wagenaar (KPN Research), Marc de Vliegher (Origin), Gerrit de Vries (Technical Union). You have been more than just helpful! This trip would not have been possible without the help of ir. Adriaan Ligtenberg (A3 Ventures), prof. Jim Senn and prof. Dick Welke (Georgia State University) and prof. Benn Konsynski (Emory Business School, Atlanta). Thank you for the enormous support. Thank you also to Ken Shain (then Cyco International, Atlanta) for helping in numerous ways! And thank you to so many American companies to be patient with our intense questioning of digital business technologies and how you are applying these in your own organisations.

We have tortured the English language in creating this text. Chris Kemp acted as its surgeon and healer. And Nancy Foy Cameron subjected our work to intense scrutiny to sharpen it up and make it accessible. Al Dunn must acknowledge an early mentor, the late Philip H. Dorn (Phil) of New York who, some twenty years ago, explained how humour is the most effective communications vehicle and that the power of common sense can overcome all confusion.

Preface

Many managers ask a compelling and difficult question: 'How can certain organisations act effectively and decisively as the digital world reshapes the ways in which business is conducted?' They see their own organisations struggling within themselves to try to win and keep customers while attempting to master the uncertainties of competition, technology, and internationalisation. Others exhibit dramatic success and growth seemingly gathering loyal and satisfied customers! What is the route to their success?

In order to succeed and grow, if not survive, organisations must redefine themselves to organise for Total Action... ensuring that every activity delivers value to a named customer. Digital business technologies enable this capability. But the technology alone is insufficient. It can do more harm than good. Rather than ensuring actions for the success of the customer, technology can amplify the organisations failings – and make them very visible to those customers. Such *Fatal Inaction* will be the killer disease of many of today's organisations. It is revealed by failure with the customer. It can be seen in intense activities which have no relationship whatsoever to an organisation's performance with that customer or for itself. Many [if not most] organisations have distanced themselves from the customer. Over time they have fragmented into discrete specialist functions and departments to manage, maintain and develop their operations and business.

Such organisations become dysfunctional. Although staffed by highly intelligent people, they become trapped in corporate autism: inward facing operating with internal markets with rules and behavioural standards that are far too rigid for the digital business world. A hard, impenetrable skin forms between the action at the front line – the sales force – and the internal organisation. The front line is disempowered, frustrated and demotivated by the failure of the 'back office' and the 'back office' is largely oblivious to the dangers of the external world of the customer.

This book shows such organisations how to assess and take charge of these failings and, by engaging with their customers, move out of Fatal Inaction to transform into Total Action: to win customers in the digital world. The book provides a road map illustrated by live examples showing how these organisations – and their management – can take the key steps by using their existing resources to form a continuing healthy relationship with their customers.

Our goal is to show how organisations can focus back on the reality of the customer – to capture their needs and respond to them effectively. 'Think customer' is not sufficient: 'act customer' must be paramount. Total Action is much more than a concept or mindset – it is a series of tools which force attention on the customer in terms of winning business and fulfilling requirements. Digital business technologies, used effectively, ensure that the information needed for every individual and team action for customer success is instantly available.

This book is a result of our work in large organisation where so many managers at every level feel trapped by the inability of the 'organisation' to flex and respond effectively to the demands of the digital world. Managers who see and begin to understand that they must capture the customer in new ways and must organise to deliver more effectively. But they cannot take the first steps!

Total Action is for the strategists – trying to steer their supertanker organisations in increasingly uncertain and uncharted seas. It is for the implementers who must translate strategies – and beliefs – into action in complex and unresponsive internal markets with conflicting and contradictory demands. It is for the IT experts who must marry the new business technologies and business possibilities with their museums of systems and behaviour. Because we have educated and trained so many, this book is also for those who have the important responsibility to develop the capabilities of the people to perform effectively in the digital world.

One goal has been to provide the missing link between the chief executive and that all-important individual customer: between the sales front and the back offices and factories. To ensure that the new business technologies do not confuse and threaten – rather they allow organisations to work outside-in and engage everyone in creating success for each customer and therefore, themselves.

Peter Vervest, Amersfoort, The Netherlands
Al Dunn, Chorleywood, England

Contents

Table of Figures

'Survival is not mandatory,
you do have a choice'

ANONYMOUS JAPANESE BUSINESS MAN

1   The boardroom agenda

Today's new digital business technologies enable organisations to achieve near complete communications and instant access to information. This can result in enormous improvements of the performance of an organisation. However, there are many examples of failure – some of which are being discussed in this book. Too often these new technologies bring no improvement whatsoever to the sharp end of the business: where and when you meet your customer. We claim this is what the digital business technologies should allow you to do better than ever before. It is achieved in three ways:

- *making the customer the locus of decision making;*
- *unlocking information about customers;*
- *integrating the fulfilment processes.*

To be successful, a rigorous method of working outside-in to engage the whole organisation – what we call 'Total Action' – must be put in place. The benefits can be enormous. By squeezing out every activity that is not specifically important for the customer, the organisation unlocks time and energy to help it win. The intense competition of a global, interconnected, digital society will force organisations to embrace the mandates of Total Action.

1.1   Win with your customer

According to Levitt: 'The purpose of business must be to get and keep a customer.'[1] Yet organisations waste *so* much time and energy on matters that do not directly give value to the customer! Imagine a competitor who could eliminate all this waste; who would only undertake activities that had direct value for the customer; where everyone had a clear and unified view of what was important for that customer; where everyone understood what could be done particularly well to help the customer.

Don't let your competitor do it first! Today's technologies enable you to do this yourself:

- eliminate waste;
- only undertake activities that are of direct value for your customer;
- perform almost every aspect of business electronically, by linking your information and communication systems effectively.

This brings a profound change in every aspect of the management of the modern corporation. And this is the concept of Total Action: *the mandate that every activity inside an organisation must be directly linked to a named customer and must deliver value to that customer.* As digital business technologies increase the degree of communication within an organisation, it has to engage outside in: to start with the customer and to derive all activity directly from the customer points of contact.

The mandate for Total Action sounds easy. Yet it feels more difficult in practice. Many people still serve the internal customer – the one who gives them recognition or promotion. Sales and customer service departments seem to be the only ones who deal with customers. Some believe that they have no customers at all. [We will look at government departments and police forces in due course.] Some senior managers see customers merely as an interrupt to creating shareholder value. So why must you think differently?

1.2   The impact of digital business technologies

The pervasive impact of modern telecommunications is rapidly revealing itself. For instance, the Internet – post the World Wide Web – and mobile

THE TOTAL ACTION MANDATE:

EVERY ACTIVITY INSIDE THE ORGANISATION

MUST BE DIRECTLY LINKED TO A NAMED CUSTOMER

AND

MUST DELIVER VALUE TO THAT CUSTOMER

ENABLED THROUGH COMPLETE COMMUNICATION.

telephones are showing growth figures which would rank them amongst the fastest growing consumer technologies. Everyone seems to be using a mobile telephone and accessing the Internet. Innovative new applications, such as electronic commerce, are no longer a concept of the future; they have become practical and often necessary options. Electronic commerce, once just a novelty, is now the accepted way of ordering and selling. Some successful innovators claim astounding results:

– Cisco, acclaimed the world's leader in networking equipment, handled 65% of all its orders via the Internet in less than a year. When the authors interviewed Cisco in August 1998, the company handled over 65,000 electronic orders per day (approx. $ 16 million worth).
– Dell, who pioneered the concept of direct marketing and make-to-order computers, has outpaced any other computer manufacturer. The company's success is attributed to the innovative use of the Internet to sell computer equipment.[2]
– It is not just high-technology companies who enjoy the benefits of the digital business world. Amazon[3], now the world's leading bookseller, is not seen as a high-tech company, and only uses technology to contact potential customers. As a favourite of the financial analysts, Amazon was valued during 1998 at nearly double the price of the largest US bookstore company, Barnes & Noble.

So what is different? First, there is the technology: the computer and telecommunications have come together. Not only can we process information very quickly by way of a computer, we can also access that information – and the people – very quickly using advanced telecommunication. This *instant* access means that you can know almost immediately what is important to you. There is almost *'complete communication'* [a theoretical concept that every part of the system knows exactly as much as every other part]. In military or logistics terms, you have almost complete communication when you know exactly where your people and materials are at any particular moment. As result you can organise your resources much better in a minute-by-minute co-ordination.

The Port of Rotterdam, for example, is the largest in the world. It has installed advanced telecommunications to co-ordinate the many discrete logistics events required to load and unload containers from ships onto trucks. One system is CargoCard, which recognises truck drivers' fingerprints as they check in at the vast port. This gives immediate knowledge on the location of the driver, truck and container in order to direct the driver to the right location. If you load and unload a ten thousand containers a day from ships, it pays to know where the trucks and the drivers are.

Only a few companies have begun to explore the impact of 'nearly complete communications' on their business. Companies like Amazon and Dell, as we will see later, understood some basic customer concepts for a digital world:

- The computer's mouse gives customers instant access to any potential supplier, world-wide. The digital customer is better informed, can be more critical, and will be more promiscuous. By pointing the mouse on the screen and clicking through the options, the customer can make instant choices. The relationship with the supplier is much looser.
- To retain the customer, you have to create new 'value'. The service elements which surround the core product are increasingly important. You need a deeper understanding of customer motives. *Why* the

customer buys may be more important than *what* the customer buys. As a supplier you must therefore organise perceived value around your core offering. For Amazon the key questions were: Why does this customer buy this book? What more value can we derive from this understanding?

– At every point of customer contact [be it digital, physical, or other] the supplier must 'know' the customer. Behind the various 'counters' where customers access suppliers, the suppliers need to have unified knowledge of relevant previous encounters as well as any other preferences or events that might help the relationship.

This is what Amazon has done for the book world. It happens with compact discs, computers, cameras, cars, art, flowers, and so forth. It will deeply impact traditional services such as insurance and financial services. As a senior bank manager told a 1996 conference:

> 'In the not too distant future a disgruntled customer will be able to click on an icon and transfer his account immediately to another bank.'[4]

Don't be misled: the challenge is not about opening an electronic counter for your customers, a site on the Internet, another call centre. This is about what happens inside your organisation: How do you engage everyone in your organisation for this specific and named customer? How do you ensure that the necessary economies of scale are still maintained while serving the individual customer?

1.3   What makes it so difficult?

History gets in the way. Look at the attraction of the small, start-up company. Everyone is new. People expect success. The company has no history, no dictate on how things must be done. People feel the entrepreneurial buzz, the sense of immediacy. Everything revolves around the main thing and keeping the main thing the main thing: *win the customer* and *win the customer again.*

  – How do we get customers – those people who pay more for what we offer than it costs us to produce?
  – How do we show people, again and again, that we can create value for them, to retain their business?
  – How do we make these strangers believers, to trust us and ultimately bring us new business and new customers?

Only few start-ups make the breakthrough. As the start-up company grows, it becomes more complex. It no longer seems so obvious that everything revolves around the customer. An internal logic develops:

 'This is the way we do things; this is our style; it has worked in the past so it will work in the future.'

The clear link between what is important to the customer and what is done internally becomes obscured. It is blurred by an internal compelling thought process which is so powerful, so strong, that it is incomprehensible for those who were there at the birth of the company.

Corporate autism
In this tower of Babel the customer is distanced from the company's decision-making processes by layers and functional divisions. All have their own cultures, their own languages and their own ambitions that diverge from those of the corporation. Individuals quickly develop inward-facing behaviour, because that's where their rewards lie. Their behaviour seems highly intelligent to themselves but has little or no significance for others. This desperate situation, so common in large organisations and so similar to human autism, is what we call 'corporate autism'. We will discuss it in greater depth in chapter 3.

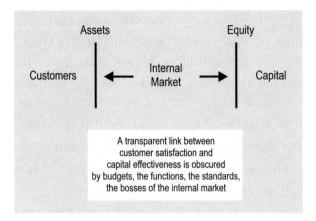

Fig. 1.1. Barriers between customers and companies

It is easy to find internal reasons or scapegoats: failing leadership, poor communications, or incorrect organisational structure. While these can contribute to the difficulties, they are not the true problem. After all, they can be changed. They are, in fact, a result of that rigorous inner logic which has become so strong, so overwhelming, that a good reason can always be given to explain why the organisation acts as it does.

Fatal inaction

Let us explore what 'corporate autism' can mean in a digital world. Imagine that you have bought a brand new car. On its maiden trip it breaks down, in the middle of the night, in the middle of nowhere. With today's technologies, the car manufacturer and the dealer could know instantly when something has gone wrong. With your car navigation system and mobile telephone transmitting the car status and position, they could immediately act to get help to you.

But whose customer are you? The car manufacturer? The dealer? The car navigation supplier? The telephone company? The car breakdown service? At that point in the night you don't care. Anyone who helps is welcome. Anyone who helps will get your custom! *And anyone who doesn't is likely to lose it.* Many parties may have access to the information that you are stranded 12 miles from the nearest garage in your brand new car. But few act in a way that is of value to you. Digital business technologies present the ability to 'know', but unless the knowledge results in useful action, the technology has done the customer no good.

"Not my fault!" some of your potential helpers say. Or "I thought *they* were taking care of that." Those who could be aware of your plight have myopic mindsets. Digital business technologies won't change mindsets; they will simply amplify the effects of fatal inaction.

Another example[5] : England's largest supermarket offers grocery shopping via the Internet. All Internet orders are printed out at headquarters, hand-carried to the fax, faxed to the store nearest the customer, where someone hand-picks the ordered goods from the shop's shelves, stands in the queue to record them, and puts them in a van for home delivery. From the customer's viewpoint, the process is convenient [providing no mistakes were made], but like the image of a serene swan, the underwater organisation is paddling wildly, spending a great deal of unnecessary energy to keep the serene image intact. The mindset is willing, but the technology use is weak.

To win in the digital world, you must develop new ways of *engaging* your organisation. Total inaction results when you know, but do not act. Fatal inaction results when you don't know and you don't act. Most companies are gradually aware of the potential of digital business technologies. However, they typically fail to adapt their organisations to take advantage of the new opportunities.

Before everything else companies must preserve or restore the basic business invariant: *every activity must be aimed at satisfying a customer in a cost-effective way*. Restoring the transparent link between customer satisfaction and capital effectiveness is fundamental for the Total Action organisation.

Some of the particular difficulties which companies encounter are:

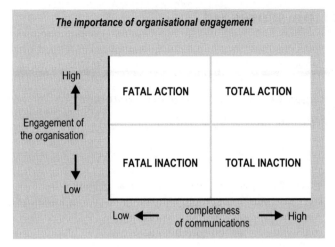

Fig. 1.2. Communication * engagement = Total Action

- failing, company-wide, to understand what the technologies can, and cannot, do;
- failing to master the new technologies;
- creating and cherishing new businesses around the customer;
- seemingly cannibalising the present business;
- changing the business metrics;
- developing new relationships with business partners.

1.4   The Total Action scorecard

For the key directors who are setting an organisation's strategy, the real questions must start with the organisation's current performance with and for the customer. As a senior manager you have to ask:

- Is my organisation's current performance adequate? Do knowledge of the customer and customer activities lead our agenda and our behaviour with the customer?
- Is this knowledge communicated, made available and acted upon? Do we support complete communications and instant access to information?

The Total Action scorecard

The customer agenda: to what extent are customer activities leading the internal agenda?

1. Most of my time is spent on customer issues.
2. I know what the customer requires.
3. I understand what we can do for this customer.
4. I understand what we plan to do for this customer.
5. I know who within our organisation takes prime responsibility for this customer.
6. I know my role and contribution to satisfying the customer.
7. We deliver good value for the customer, much better than our competitors.
8. The customer believes that we deliver good value.
9. My manager believes that we receive good value from this customer.
10. I do not undertake activities that are not of value to the customer.

Score each question on a scale of 1 to 5.
1=strongly disagree; 2=disagree; 3=neutral; 4=agree; 5=totally agree.

Interactive capabilities: how well do they support complete communications and instant access to information?

1.   We know everything we need to know about this customer.

2.   We have accurate data on our performance with this customer.

3.   Information on the customer is always up to date and complete.

4.   I can easily access the information that we hold on this customer.

5.   I can easily access the people within the organisation responsible for this customer.

6.   The customer can always contact us.

7.   We know about all contacts that the customer has with us.

8.   We analyse customer information regularly as the basis of improving our services.

9.   All departments as well as our business partners have access to the same information on this customer.

10. Our management tries to give everyone instant access to the customer information which is relevant to them.

The *Total Action scorecard* can be used as a checklist to generate a clear diagnosis, so the strategy can bridge the gap between what the organisation is, and what you want it to be.

Scoring your organisation

To use the *Total Action scorecard* ask a number of representative customers to name those people in your organisation who are directly or indirectly involved in serving them. Then plot the wider chain of people and functions involved in the customer service cycle for each customer.

Ask all those identified to answer the questions on the two cards, and score their answers 1 to 5. Once you have a measure of where you are, you can plan where you want to be, and how you are going to get there.

We believe the steps to Total Action summarised in figure 1.3 and amplified in the rest of this book, will help take you where you want to go.

- *make the customer the locus of decision-making* — organise customer leaders and customer action teams;
- *ensure access to customer information* — enhance interactive capabilities with effective information platforms and customer dashboards;
- *manage fulfilment by integral management of the demand chain* in the organisation's *value web* [business network].

The organisation's perception of the customer changes, often dramatically, as it implements the Total Action approach. People begin to see that the technology enables them to add more value for the customer [or in some cases to accept that they actually have customers]. As a result they can re-position and strengthen themselves in the value chain, and increase job satisfaction. In the cases of the police and postal organisations described in chapter 4, major shifts in management approach

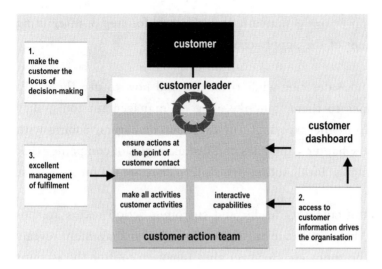

Fig. 1.3. The Total Action model

come with the recognition of the customer and the process of creating customer value. Total Action has also changed IT priorities to designing and developing the abilities of the customer dashboard.

Many organisations have found that digital business technologies demand a far better internal management and co-ordination of customer data. You won't gain very much by opening web sites if can't develop or maintain a unified view of the customer.

1.5   The Total Action model

This book includes a number of tools that can help your company develop and implement a strategy for Total Action, using digital business technologies to renew the spirit of a start–up innovator, engaging from outside-in to make the customer, once again, the centre of everything you do. These tools include:

- the customer leader and the customer action team [tools for step 1, making the customer the locus of decision making];
- the customer dashboard [a tool for step 2, accessing customer information];

– the modular business network design [a tool for step 3, integrating management of the supply chain].

Chapters 2 and 3 describe what these are and how to use them. We have put names to them, but like all good management tools, they really come from the experience of excellent managers, coping with real problems. Chapter 4 includes detailed examples of companies that have tried to apply Total Action principles. They are set out in a 'case study' format.

The concepts of customer leader and customer action teams are not entirely new. Much literature on sales and account management reveals the basics of the approach. However, they too often confine the account manager to the role of super-sales person. Such account managers have too few tools to find, and therefore use, essential customer information. Nor are they mandated to form customer teams to drive outside-in methods into the organisation.

The importance of integrated management of the supply chain cannot be overstated. But the initial effort of building the raw model for each of the business partners can seem prohibitive. It often requires detailed process diagrams to develop and demonstrate alternative designs. Then the key importance of fulfilment becomes very clear. The issues surrounding fulfilment [uniform definition of key processes, sharing vital transaction data, and common command and control] can then be addressed.

The most emotional aspects of embedding Total Action are usually the intensive effort on the part of top executives to start 'engaging outside-in'. Some people, conditioned by years of successful internal focus, have difficulty responding to the simple logic of 'putting the customer first'. While doing this, an executive has to satisfy the demands of top management for improved earnings.

1.6   Questions from the board

How do you measure interactive capability? Or corporate autism?
This is not easy. Two of the most common questions are on the scorecard: *to what extent are customer activities leading the internal agenda? And how well are interactive capabilities developed to support complete communications and instant access to information?*
The measurement methods are still somewhat arbitrary, and need your experienced judgement to interpret them. The Total Action scorecard can help, but its objective is not an exact determination. Rather it is to gain significant improvement of the present performance. Fatal inaction is easier to measure than Total Action – it is certainly easier to see, as a customer. Even so, a relative improvement on today's performance – determined according to customer criteria – can open untapped potential.

If you surrender your organisation in this way to the customer, will you ever make money?
You do not 'surrender' your organisation to any dictate of any customer. You can say 'no' to any customer request. The important point is that most organisations don't even *hear* the customer requests, much less say no; they simply tamper with the issue, take an excessive time to take a decision, fail to inform the customer in case the customer is upset, and basically make it very difficult and frustrating for the customer – and for themselves.
Not all customers bring equal profit – or 'value' – to the company. This can be the basis for discriminating between services to different customers – but you can't do this if you don't understand how much of that customer's business you have [and vice versa], or what the company's goals with the customer should be. Without reliable data, how can you decide?
As a matter of definition, there are no unprofitable customers. There are, however, unprofitable ways of serving a customer. The customer

can always be profitable but if your company chooses to serve him the wrong way, or fails to gain extra benefit from the opportunities of each customer contact, it's your own fault, not the customer's.

We ask too much of our people; they cannot do this!

We believe that human resource management and training must combine. They must provide a much more rigorous assessment of individuals and their management, with sophisticated computer-supported environments for action training.

We also believe that most managers, especially in the middle layers of large organisations, underestimate the potential of their people. In our experience they tend to stifle the thinking and behaviour of their employees, hemming them in with inadequate communication and over-detailed delegation. The person the manager says is unfit to meet a customer may be managing the tennis club in his spare time.

Total Action is a way of engaging more of everyone's abilities in real, customer-related actions. Employees naturally want to win, to be successful with customers. As a result of a rigorous outside-in approach, managers and employees all have a better chance to achieve this success. The failure of recruitment and induction processes is more serious. Too often new and inexperienced managers are recruited from outside the industry to revitalise an organisation. This may appear necessary, but the induction – the translation of their capabilities into organisational value – must be done with extreme care.

Isn't this just another plea for empowerment?

In part, yes. The essence of empowerment is to give the people who do the job the power and tools they need to do the job properly. Total Action is about linking every customer activity in the organisation, removing activities that aren't relevant to the customer, and letting customer teams and customer leaders take on power themselves. Empowering the customer leaders and their customer action teams is clearly important. But it isn't sufficient to deliver the performance improvement. Total Action demands that this improvement comes from eliminating unnecessary activities and embarking on new, more promising ones. Access to information is crucial. Unless information is easily communicated, Total Action cannot work.

How does Total Action differ from 'core competence' and 'strategic intent'?

Defining your core competence is not trivial – this analysis is very important for the modern firm. But what is a core competence in practice? In Total Action the customer is taken as the reference point. Core competence theory claims that this emphasis may be too restrictive. The present customer may not be a good direction for future competitive competencies. We disagree! Customer leaders and customer action teams are well able to distinguish the customer needs – now and in future – from their more pressing and immediate needs or their wants.

We believe the Total Action view on portfolio and supply chain management complements core competence theory. And we are convinced that the skills developed for Total Action will be pivotal for future competence development, both for individuals and for their companies.

We are already doing this. What's new?

Many organisations are doing parts of Total Action. But few actually bring together all its constituent parts:

- the customers as the locus of decision-making;
- customer information;
- supply chain management; and
- working outside-in.

To bring these together – in parallel and linked – is new for most organisations. Juran[6] and Crosby[7] encountered similar responses when they advocated TQM as a way to embed quality in the full process of specification, design, procurement, materials management, production, marketing, sales and service. Rather than something done by the quality department, quality becomes a process, with a defined process owner and a common acceptance throughout the organisation. Total Action can have a similar effect, taking responsibility for customers beyond the Sales people, to make customer interaction a cohesive, recognisable process that engages the whole organisation.

What role should the marketing and sales departments have?

In our experience, marketing and sales are usually the first to embrace the concepts of Total Action. As in the quality example, this is an opportunity to widen recognition of what they do, and how important the rest of the organisation is to their success.

Rather than meeting specific raw sales targets, the sales force should emerge as a high-tech and professional group managing customer relationships. Sales people are not simply an 'outlet to the market' who understand how to swing a deal and rid the organisation of its excess inventory. The sales process has to be defined more clearly as the full set of customer interactions to manage the service cycle. Sales defines how the customer interaction processes will work and which information dashboards are needed. The IT departments must then put these in place. Too often we find that sales is not taking a pro-active role and is not spelling out customer-related requirements to the technical IT people.

Marketing, too, gains a new dimension. It can gather intelligence on the various customer groups through the structured and planned interactions of customer leaders and customer action teams. Marketing requires more agility in analysis of the historical data on the customers, and on the performance of the organisation, the plans of the customer leaders and the plans of product management and manufacturing. This analysis can yield masses of data to support sales as well as feeding the planning of the company processes. Note that this makes operational field data a formidable source of advantage. Some companies are already doing this in cycle times of less than 24 hours!

Our IT systems will never be able to support this.
Fix them! Despite all the promise of the digital business technologies, many organisations are still trapped in their computer museums, with outdated processes, and an overloaded agenda from the IT director. There is light at the end of the tunnel. We have had some good experiences of 'outside-in' automation. The customer leaders and their customer action teams define their information and communication requirements, which they can satisfy by simple, off-the-shelf support software. Marketing and sales bosses, and often the marketing communication directors too, prefer rapid prototyping to long tedious overhauls of complete IT warehouses. It is very important that marketing and sales take an interest, if not budget-control, over the IT spend for their activities.

So what must we do first?
Measure your interactive capabilities, benchmark them against those of your competitors or other industries. Find out how they do it differently. Above all, analyse the interaction processes with your customers and seek to assess your Total Action score. We offer no generic recipe to assess your position and what you must do next. However, we feel that it is relatively straightforward to determine your own score. Then you have to draw on the experiences and knowledge of your own organisation, particularly the front line, and those of your customers. They'll tell you how well your technical infrastructure stands up in comparison with your competitors – if they think you really want to know.
At the heart of the Total Action challenge is general agreement that something must be done – and it can be done. This is a change that everyone wants: your customers, your employees, your shareholders, your managers, yourselves.

2 Digital business technologies and Total Action

Those organisations that can take full advantage of digital business technologies will have the greatest opportunity to gain sustainable advantage over competitors. But they will bear little resemblance to the traditional organisations that surround us today. Speed and customer-focused responsiveness will be their watchwords.

Electronic linkages have fundamentally changed the world and will impact the whole of commerce. Organisations in a web of instant communication can act faster to serve their customers. Functional organisations will disintegrate, to be replaced by others that centre on customer processes.

Digital business technologies are evolving faster than the average organisation can absorb them. Consequently, the future of digital business is being shaped by fast-moving, innovative young organisations. Large, traditional organisations must learn from them and emulate the best of their behaviour. Otherwise, tomorrow's customer will click the mouse and move to a competitor.

2.1 The new digital business technologies

We have seen a major and dramatic change in combining and using digital business technologies. There is a true revolution in the collection, manipulation, storage, presentation and communication of information, whether it be speech, text, pictures, audio, or video. Information that was traditionally stored on paper, in photographs, or in audio and videotape can now be translated into a series of 'zeros' and 'ones' or

DIGITAL BUSINESS TECHNOLOGIES ARE

THE INTEGRATED INFORMATION AND COMMUNICATIONS SYSTEMS

— COMPUTERS, TELEPHONES AND TELEVISIONS —

THAT ENABLE THE ELECTRONIC PERFORMANCE OF BUSINESS,

LINKING INDIVIDUALS, BUSINESSES,

AND OTHER ORGANISATIONS.

'digital bits' that can be handled by omnipresent microchips. This seemingly simple capability has created entirely new markets and industries – and it is redefining the ways in which business can be conducted.

Digital business technologies are pervasive

Digital capabilities are invading common place goods and services. They have given the simple *telephone* an impressive range of functions.

- It can redirect calls to another telephone.
- It can reveal the telephone number of your caller.
- It travels in your pocket or briefcase.
- Your mobile telephone can now receive faxes and text messages.
- Every time you turn your mobile on, the system knows where the telephone is.
- It has acquired a small keyboard and is becoming a computer.
- At the same time, your computer is becoming a very agile telephone.

The Internet makes the power of these new digital business technologies combinations highly visible. At home or at work you can use your *computer* to watch television, listen to the radio, download video or audio tracks, read a newspaper, plan a trip, shop, or search for information about your specific interests. You can order a new bit of software, a book, flowers, or chocolates. The Internet can deliver the digital products, and it can even convert the book into digital format and deliver it directly to your computer. The Internet needs a middleman, though, to get physical products like chocolates or flowers to you in good condition.

Your *credit card* is becoming a smart card. Digital cash can be stored on it over the telephone network or from an automatic teller machine [ATM or 'hole in the wall'] connected to your bank through the telephone network. The smart card can carry your personal details, your medical records or your regular purchases at the supermarket.

Your *digital television* can record your viewing habits, providing a rich information base for advertising as well as informing you that a preferred programme is scheduled.

Digital business technologies are truly social technologies. Electronic mail [or *'e-mail'*] has become a dominant way to communicate in many organisations. Unmanaged, it expands, causing stress for over-busy people struggling through hundreds of disjointed messages and incompatible attachments every day. At the same time, e-mail is becoming a social application as rapidly increasing numbers of individuals communicate computer-to-computer over the Internet. Teenagers send text messages between mobile telephones. The family can now send messages [with photographs attached] between television screens. Long-lost cousins find each other through genealogy forums.

The Internet has demonstrated how easily individuals throughout the world can link together and communicate. They form common-interest groups. They jump in and out of information sources. [It is, perhaps, no coincidence that much of the vocabulary of the Internet is social rather than business. Business people do not 'surf' – they enquire and research!] As the ability to process, store, and communicate digital information, is embedded into personal devices, new behaviour and expectations are being generated. New communication channels such as telephone ordering and payment have enriched [or endangered] the traditional relationship between consumers and suppliers. The speed

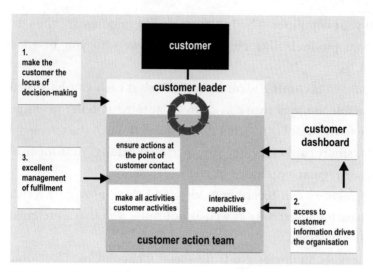

Fig. 2.1. The attributes of digital business technologies

and flexibility possible at the sales front must now be married to equivalent abilities inside the organisation.

The attributes of digital business technologies

The digital business technologies world appears complex. As in the 1980's world of computers and telecommunication, there is a complex technical vocabulary and a confusion of products and application. Yet the basic ability of these technologies is 'digitisation' – converting text, sound, picture or any other kind of information – into a stream of zeros and ones. This single concept underpins the tremendous importance these technologies are gaining in both social and business life. Digital business technologies have two capabilities that underpin the transformation of the business world, they 'disconnect' information from its physical form and from geography.

Physical disconnection — information which previously existed only on paper, on magnetic audio or video tape, or on photographic material in 'analogue' [non-digital] form can now exist as a 'bit stream' of zeroes and ones, the digits which can be stored and processed electronically.

The photograph can now be created directly in digital format with a digital camera. An analogue picture can be converted into digital format using a 'scanner'. Then you can process it, manipulate it, edit it, change its colours, put Aunt Minnie's head on Elvis's body. Similarly you can manipulate or edit voice, graphics, and video. Driven by continuing improvements in the price/performance of hardware for processing and storage, *image processing* has made it as easy to deal with images as it is to use text and data. As a result, we are now becoming adapt at dealing with *compound digital documents*, made up of individual 'objects' – text, data, image, etc. You can build and edit your church newsletter or community poster on the screen, then check it over with others on line before you print it. As you create the page on the computer, you can easily edit and re-structure letters, words and paragraphs. With a few clicks of the mouse, you can incorporate a drawing, a photo-graph or even a symbol that accesses a voice or video object. As soon as you commit the page to paper, though, you lose all these capabilities: it becomes analogue information.

Geographical disconnection — when you can not only transform information but also send it around the world, the impact of digitisation is profound. The objects on the digital page can live on a computer or storage device anywhere in the world and you can bring them together to create that particular page. Then you can send it to another computer, somewhere else, where it can undergo further transformations. Two or more people, anywhere in the world, can work simultaneously on the document. You can broadcast it, sending it to millions of recipients with a few strokes of the keyboard. Or, in reverse, many individuals can access your document from anywhere.

Digital business technologies remove distance as an information constraint. Without communication, the value of information – even in digital form – is seriously constrained. Islands of information, trapped in expensive old technology behind departmental and functional walls, have become a barrier to the free flow of information within and between organisations.

The Internet and its progeny are making information a world-wide collective commodity just as we begin to understand the value of information as a collective asset. As we move towards the time when everyone has immediate access to the same information, the traditional advantage of the information edge is beginning to leak away. The gap between 'haves' and 'have-nots' is narrowing. It used to be the case that 'those who have the information have the power'. Today it is becoming 'those who can access the information have the power'.

The Internet: accessing and linking

Information cannot exist in a vacuum. The age-old question is: 'When a tree falls in the forest, when there is no one to hear it, does it make a noise?' Access and linking are as important, if not more important, than the information itself.

The Internet unfreezes the vast archives of digital information that exist throughout the world. It has demonstrated the power of the *linking* of information and of *access* to information. The Internet has a critical strength: anyone anywhere can access and link to digital information. Until the mid 90s it was a wild information jungle with basic tools that allowed only experienced users to search for and exchange information. The emergence of the World Wide Web and web browsers has improved these capabilities dramatically.

The World Wide Web introduced electronic pointers or links that connect information in one 'server' ['client-server' or shared computer] to another, using 'hypermedia'. For example, in a hypermedia document clicking on the coloured and underscored word 'hypermedia' would link you to another document somewhere in the world – giving a detailed explanation of that word. You need no knowledge about the location or address of this location.

Such a link can bring you to a file containing audio, graphics, or video.

This creates the non-linear or 'webbed' information world of the Internet. 'Browsers' then created an easy-to-use window on the Internet world, presenting menus from which your information routes or activities can be selected. These tools, and those that continue developing from them, provide the substantial capabilities now available for organising, accessing and presenting digital information.

2.2   Why are digital business technologies so important?

What's different? Why do we have to take digital business technologies so seriously today when they have attracted so much lip service in the past?

2.2.1   *New ways to reach customers*

Customers who begin using digital access channels – particularly the Internet – are finding new routes to their suppliers. Their expectations are rising, and their demands are becoming more stringent. Even those who remain on the more traditional conduits, including the telephone, are beginning to show the same expectations of rapid, if not instant, gratification. [Once Viking Direct has sent your printer cartridge overnight, you grow impatient with another firm that needs five days to take care of you.]

Few organisations are truly prepared for the impact of digital business technologies. Tokenism will not be sufficient. Erecting a 'digital window' to the world without establishing the necessary organising capabilities will magnify any organisational weaknesses and will risk losing customers.

These changes do not apply only to those who interface directly to the consumer. Those further back up the supply chain will also need to adapt their behaviour to meet the needs of their direct customers. Only when they focus on the customer's customer can they really fulfil the requirements of the direct customer.

Digital business technologies widen the scope of access for customers;

they also widen the opportunities to learn *about* customers. Vital data on the customer can be captured and acted upon. Digital channels, particularly the telephone, have increasingly augmented the familiar physical channels to the customer. The Internet now provides a further channel. Interactive digital television and other access technologies will increase the channels available to and about customers.

Usually organisations talk of *'outlets'* for their goods or services. This reflects the inside-out thinking of shifting inventory to the customer. With digital capabilities, these channels become two-way. They can be *'inlets'* for knowledge about the customer and the marketplace.

Amazon: bookshop for the digital customer

Amazon claims to be the largest bookshop in the world. It is a digital shop on the Internet. Amazon's customer access is a web site[1]. When you revisit the site, it remembers your previous visits and your interests. It welcomes you by name and suggests new books that might interest you, based on your history.

If you are seeking a particular book, you can type what you know about that book: author, title or subject. The system checks its availability a list of 3 million titles. [The largest Barnes & Noble superstore can only hold 175,000 books.] Amazon tells you whether the book you want can be sent immediately, or that it may take a week or more.

If you are browsing Amazon's web page, the system makes it easy and interesting. You can explore specific subject areas and look at relevant books and reviews.

If you decide to order, an electronic order form helps you decide how and where, and how quickly to send the book. For a known customer, payment is straightforward. When the book has been sent Amazon tells you by e-mail. If the book is difficult to find it e-mails you when it is available. For completely customised service, Amazon is working with its main book distributor, Ingram Book Group, to deliver books order by order.

The Amazon system helps you e-mail the author or the publisher if you wish. You can read reviews from magazines and other readers, and you can add your own comments.

You never speak to a person, yet the web site is more informative than a person. And, of course, Amazon learns much more about you than if you bought the book in a normal bookshop. Amazon learns not only the identity of the customer, but also the books bought, topics of interest, search behaviour, buying frequency, etc.

A few statistics are illuminating. With 1997 sales of $148 million [an almost ten-fold increase on 1996] Amazon employees brought in some $250, 000 each [over twice the industry average]. The company has 1.5 million customer accounts, with half the purchases being repeats. Amazon has no retail store space. Its inventory is about 2% of that of Barnes & Noble. It discounts some 400,000 books, cutting paperback prices by 20% and hardbacks by 30%. For the UK buyer, the savings are of the order of 40%. Amazon also has an excellent cash flow advantage. When you buy the book, Amazon collects from your credit card immediately. It then pays the book publishers 45 days later.

More than this, through agreements with other web sites, Amazon can attract potential buyers to its site. For example, when you visit the official Bob Dylan web site it links you to Amazon to look at the Bob Dylan books that are available. Increasingly other sites around the Internet are providing a logical access to Amazon, related to their own subject matter. This is a very powerful base from which the Amazon can market books and expand to other related products and services that their customers may want. For example, you can now buy CDs from Amazon.

Amazon is a *digital company*. It exists only on the Internet as far as the customer is concerned. It is able to reduce the costs of selling books to the public and organise their delivery extremely effectively. Its share value has grown much faster than any of the 'traditional' booksellers and it has made serious inroads into their market shares. Amazon has already changed the book business in two fundamental ways:

- book distribution is becoming a global business, breaking out of the confines of national boundaries and their associated conventions;
- Amazon has created a new and effective way of buying and selling books.

Is Amazon better than the average 'physical' bookshop? It is certainly different and, for many book buyers, very attractive. There will still be many desiring the touch and feel of the traditional shop. By amassing valuable information, Amazon serves the customer in entirely new ways. It reduces the cost of customer interaction dramatically while improving its usefulness. Amazon still must make sure it attracts new customers – hooking new customers to the system will probably be its biggest challenge. But once you enter its digital self-service environment you, as a customer, are in charge! You, the customer, are the locus of decision-making. Amazon has full access to the most valuable customer information:

- who reads what;
- how often do they buy;
- do they have specialist interests; and
- how do they search?

Similarly, Dell Computers has seized the opportunities of digital business technologies to establish a robust position in the PC marketplace and steal business from more traditional competitors.

Dell Computer: modules make it easy

When you visit Dell Computer's web site[2], you can configure and buy a personal computer, pay for it and, over the following days, check the order and its delivery status. Purchasing a PC can be complex process. Dell makes it straightforward by eliminating distributors and guiding the buyers through structured choices that can then be combined into the desired PC. The product and the necessary services are constructed

based on the customer's selection of individual standardised modules.
Dell has made it very easy to buy the computer.

The company founded its successful business by bringing new thinking
to bear on how customers buy products. Dell began with the conviction
that customers would buy PCs by mail order. These could then be assembled
to order, from mass-produced components. This approach eliminated the
traditional PC dealers whom the company regarded as an inefficient and
error-prone interface with the customer. Dell felt that without the dealer
in between, the company could be closer and more responsive to its
customer.

In September 1993, Dell augmented its initial direct mail order buying
by setting up a major international telephone centre in Ireland, providing
direct sales and support to customers. Though many regarded this as a
foolish move, the company's European sales grew by 28% in the first
quarter of 1994. In January 1997, Dell began sales over the Internet. As
a result, Dell's PC sales increased by more than 70% in 1998, well above
the industry average of 11%. In 14 years, Michael Dell has built a $12
billion company.

Dell is reducing costs and can offer competitive prices. On Dell's web
page, for example, customers have the task of keying in information which,
previously, had to be done by Dell people. Rather than the customer
telephoning the 'help desk' to check the status of a delivery and thus,
tying up phone lines and Dell people, the customer is able to check
directly on Dell's internal systems. Dell has removed inventory from its
customer channels and ensures tight management of the remaining
inventory. Dell is also closer to information about the customer and,
consequently, is able to improve its forecasting and derive more knowledge
about customer requirements. Today, through the web, and previously
through its telephone ordering systems, the company has been able to
feed customer information directly back into product and service design.
For example, in 1991, Dell, acting on customer feedback, was the first
to offer free installation of applications software as a standard service
option.

In addition, Dell is targeting its major corporate customers through the web. It has created some 1,500 home pages, tailored for each of its largest customers, giving them direct access to corporate PC configurations. They can use the pages to negotiate discounts and track their purchases and payments[3]. This makes traditional levels of services unacceptable. Why would a buyer go through traditional ordering procedures, to find limits on the customisation and wait longer for shipment.

Amazon and Dell demonstrate that harvesting opportunities from digital business technologies involves more than 'establishing a web presence'. They know that the organisation must act 'internally' – it must organise – to deliver better products or services to their customers.

When an organisation puts responsive capabilities at the front-line, using a web page or call centre, it has to live up to the response it promises, so internal performance has to be streamlined as well. Otherwise customers find it easy to migrate.

You only have to ask

In 1997, a survey of those UK financial institutions wishing to demonstrate their interactive capabilities by having a web presence produced the following results.[4]

Whenever this web presence urged the visitor to e-mail for further information, the survey organisation sent such an e-mail. The majority of the organisations, – well over 90% – never responded to the e-mails. The few who did responded very slowly, in many cases weeks later.

When these financial companies were asked [by telephone, not by e-mail] why their responses had been nil or too slow, the main reason given was: "It was too difficult to answer the questions." Some also said it was too expensive. They said it cost over £10 [$18] for each response.

Why did they ask for e-mails in the first place? Having discovered the difficulty and expense of responding, why did they not stop doing it? Why not introduce a simple checklist of questions that would direct those interested into answering questions that the institutions could answer with ease?

In 1998, it was reported that the banking community was moving slowly in Internet use. A survey of 100 of the leading banks in over 25 countries found that 96% did not expect to increase revenue from online transactions. No figures were reported on any resultant decline in revenue. Only 34% overall and just over half the US banks believed that the Internet would help them maintain existing customers. Very few banks had any kind of strategy for Internet banking and only a very small number had any idea of how they might generate revenue on the Internet.

The picture was similar in financial services.

The application of digital business technologies alone does not improve the performance of an organisation. In fact, new technologies can make matters worse if the organisation is not prepared for them. A customer's digital access to an organisation can reveal the latter's inherent incapability. Given the customer's ability to access the organisation quickly, slow response to that customer's requirements or the inability to fulfil the customer's needs is unacceptable.

When the inside and the outside worlds collide![5]

Tesco, the largest UK food retailer holds 45% of the market with an annual turnover of £16+ billion [$28+ billion]. Tesco has a reputation for using IT to innovate and gain competitive advantage. Tesco has been adept at building business with customers through a loyalty card system. Consequently, the company has increased market share in an intensely competitive market. In 1998, they made a relatively innovative step and introduced a home-shopping trial using the Internet. Those online customers close to the two pilot areas, London and Leeds were able to log into their home shopping site, and order items for delivery the next day.

Behind this seamless activity, the fulfilment process was *not* straight-forward. When the shopper made an online, interactive selection from a list of 22,000 items that outside world took a collision course with the world inside Tesco.

When the customer agreed the order one would have expected the electronic fulfilment chain to trigger. It did, but this was not 'world-class' electronic fulfilment. From the web site [in Hertfordshire] the order was transferred to an office block in Scotland. There it was printed out, carried by hand across the office, handed to one of 400 people in a typing pool to be keyed into a second computer system and filed for reference. The electronic copy was then send by e-mail or by fax to the shopper's local store. Again, it was printed – twice: one copy for the customer and the other for the 'picker' who then had to fight through the normal shoppers, collect the goods while ticking them off the shopping list, wait in line at the check out, pack them into boxes and then transfer them to a van which took them to the shopper's home. If the shopper was at home, the goods were delivered and paid for by cheque or credit card [with a surcharge]. No doubt, that payment then entered a separate financial chain.

For the tele-shopper who received the goods at home it worked – provided there were no manual errors [for which there is ample opportunity] in the fulfilment chain. If fact the whole cycle would be much simpler if the Internet-empowered shoppers simply faxed their orders to their local stores. But, as Paul Arnold, head of Tesco Direct, commented: 'it is possible that that would work. But it is not the way we have chosen to do it'.

2.2.2   Breakthrough – and incredible impact

The digital business technologies have actually arrived. They are here and they are having an incredible impact – whether or not your own organisation is taking account of it. That provides an immediate reason to pay attention to the technologies – and to exploit them better than your competitors do.

The concept of the information system as a competitive weapon has almost become a cliché, and for many, a disappointment. Organisations have been exploiting digital business technologies since the late 1970s. A significant proportion of organisational budgets is spent on information technology and related activities[6]. People seldom question 'Should we spend?' Instead they ask 'What is the return on our spend?' or even 'Why are we doing this?'

Many of the big promises of information technology ['IT'] have not been fulfilled. While some 'strategy success stories' are repeated, the majority of organisations have experienced the growth of monolithic IT departments, increasingly remote from the realities of business, creating a self-sufficient world which continues to demand more budget. There were high ambitions and expectations. Visionaries predicted the 'interconnected digital world' where individuals and organisations could communicate and access information with no limits on time or place. As prices fell and processing power was compacted into desktop and home personal computers, these visions were strengthened. By the mid-1980s the spotlight shifted to inter-organisational information systems. As deregulation encouraged telecommunications competition, new services began to make it possible for one organisation to link its internal processes with those of its trading partners. Data could be exchanged electronically. For many organisations, this approach was and still is successful.

As we entered the 1990s, the ability to share information between remote computers increased. However, users had to grapple with the increasing availability but limited capabilities of 'the computer and data communications'. And non-computer activities came under fire. For example, the introduction of an on-line or telephone ordering system for customers can immediately cause problems in matching orders to available inventory and ensuring delivery. The innovation puts stress on the on the back office and the supply side. Consequently, continuing cycles of 'process renewal' have to meet the increasing problems. Without excellent management of these activities, chaos – or frantic extemporisation – can result.

Parts of the supply chain have traditionally been the target of digital business technologies, normally within individual functions or

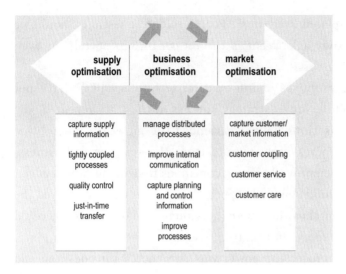

Fig. 2.2. The digital impact c. 1985 – 1995

departments. As figure 2.2 illustrates, they usually began with business optimisation [the internal processes], then moved to both market optimisation [sales and marketing systems] and supply optimisation [purchasing systems].

Widely known instances include American Airlines[7] [reservation systems], McKesson Drug Company [distribution systems], and Merrill Lynch[8] [cash management systems]. Keen[9] explores these and other examples. For many organisations the reality was more problematical:

> 'The concepts of gaining competitive advantage by linking
> organisations through information technology has taken on an
> overtone of dogma in many business circles in recent years.
> Unfortunately, the reality of developing and maintaining electronic
> linkages between companies is not as easy or as profitable as the
> optimistic preaching of interorganisational systems advocates would
> lead us to believe.'[10]

Benjamin et al. argue that this application of Electronic Data Interchange [known as 'EDI'] was not inspired by the search for competitive advantage but rather by competitive necessity: not using it means losing business. Digital business technologies become the Achilles' heel rather than the competitive edge.

Most business optimisation has taken the form of accelerating existing processes rather than redesigning the business to tap the new capabilities of digital business technologies. Supply optimisation has been a driver for business redesign in terms of close coupling with supplier processes, but, again, it has tended to accelerate existing processes ['speed up the order'].

'Too little, too early' is another pitfall. Technology has created solutions but most of them are trapped in yesterday's technologies and applications. The existing telecommunication and data platforms, together with their inflexible organisational structures and behaviours make it extremely difficult to integrate these applications even for the, seemingly straight-forward, exchange of data. In addition, with each change, the impact on other activities triggers new problems.

These approaches are too often uncoordinated. Changes in one element of a business, for example sales and marketing, place new demands on the other parts of the business. This can force organisations into continuing cycles of renewing discrete systems, without being able to achieve end-to-end integration.

Telestroika: the liberation of communications
Historically, the inflexibility of computer-to-computer communications was a major barrier to optimisation. Without rigid [usually proprietary] standards, one computer was unable to talk to another. The Internet has brought a critical characteristic which places it at the centre of the new digital business technologies: *computers of all kinds, anywhere, are able to use it and, as a result, communicate with one another.* All they need is the very basic communications software and a telephone line. In addition, the World Wide Web offers software for searching the information chaos of the Internet, and 'browsers' make it easy to

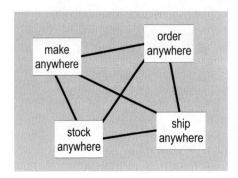

Fig. 2.3. Telestroika

use the Internet. As figure 2.3 illustrates it no longer matters where you make it, order it, stock it, or ship it. That's Telestroika!

Now, as a result, digital business technologies really *do* remove the constraints of space and time. Using the Internet, a customer in Hong Kong can order your product from a web server based in New York, triggering the downloading of software from Texas, video from Hollywood, music from Paris, or a book from Czechoslovakia. If the product has a physical form, physical fulfilment is necessary – but the customer will expect delivery very promptly. You have to remove as much time as possible from the fulfilment process.

As companies are learning, sometimes to their cost, Telestroika offers splendid opportunities, but it demands change to deep-rooted patterns. Figure 2.4 illustrates how product and information flows have to be integrated and synchronised.

An example from the automotive industry illustrates the opportunities, once systems can interchange information.

Lucas: from supplier to customer, seamlessly

This vision is not new. Towards the end of the 1980s Lucas, the UK-based automotive electronics company, was trying to realise it by implementing electronic data interchange. Lucas had implemented application-to-application communication between its customers [car

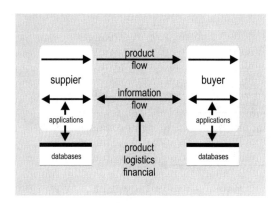

Fig. 2.4. Integrating and synchronising product and information flows

manufacturers], its manufacturing planning systems and the manufacturing systems of its component suppliers.

Lucas did not use electronic purchase orders. The company exchanged a series of schedules [date, requirements, and probability] with the car manufacturers. These were updated as the date of delivery grew closer. Consequently, Lucas planned according to the car manufacturer's requirements and ensured exact delivery, as figure 2.5 illustrates.

Lucas sent electronic invoices to the car manufacturers. These were accurate since they were based on electronic data fed in by despatch control. In parallel, the car manufacturer was able to match the invoice electronically against data from receipt control, and initiate payment. In fact, Lucas really did not need to send invoices since both parties knew what had been ordered, delivered, and accepted electronically. All they needed to do was to send the payment electronically.

2.2.3 Management has to master their use

The Lucas example linked three parties: the car manufacturer, Lucas, and its suppliers. The capabilities of a number of organisations were merged together in a *business network* to satisfy a particular customer requirement. When managers are masters, not slaves, of the technologies, they can mobilise a web of co-operating organisations, from the point of customer contact, to go into action mode for fulfilment. [The *co-*

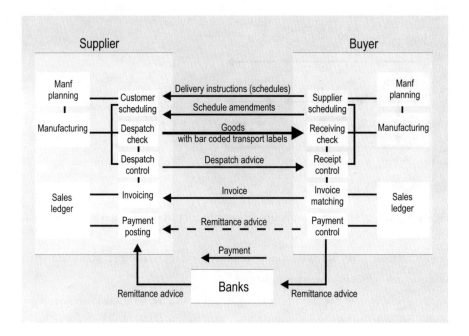

Fig. 2.5. A vision for electronic data integration

operative business network is a simple term for the seeming complexity of such terms as virtual organisations or collaborative inter-enterprise working.]

Digital business technologies enable and encourage collaboration. Individuals are able to communicate instantly with one another and they share the same information at the same time. With digital business technologies, it is nonsense for a buyer to send a purchase order, the supplier to send an invoice, the buyer to then query the invoice and eventually send a cheque. The traditional process costs too much and offers too many opportunities for mistakes. The flow of information between these organisations becomes electronic. This can be more than simply making an electronic version of the formal business documents. Instead, the applications in the two organisations can collaborate. For example, the buyer's manufacturing planning system can communicate with the supplier's manufacturing system so they act as one cohesive system.

For the managers who deploy and link them effectively, digital business technologies can communicate customer requirements instantly, and trigger the necessary action to fulfil them. The technologies also offer immediate knowledge about the status of activities. This ability to organise and manage such a rapid-action business network is a key part of Total Action. Total Action means that an organisation with its business network of trading partners and internal capabilities is able to summon *the lifetime orientation on the customer* and *fluid, self-organising capabilities.*

Lifetime orientation — the customer transaction must be more than a one-off event. The supplier must gather and interpret vital data about the history and behaviour of the customer to make sure that that customer continues to feel loyal and that the relationship can be increasingly profitable. This means that:

- knowledge on the customer must be gathered at every point of contact, and translated into action so the organisation is able to improve its performance *with* the customer [managing the relationship] and *for* the customer [delivering to requirements]; and
- the vendor must continually measure and assess the organisation's performance *with* and *for* the customer, to be able to improve performance as a result.

Many 'customer care' or 'customer loyalty' programmes force the customer to behave according to the 'rule of the business' and gather information that does not appear to be applied effectively. Consider a simple example:

You are a Gold Card passenger of a major airline. Every time you fly with them, you can share the splendour of their executive lounges and collect air miles for future free flights. You have been their VIP for some five years. You now take extended leave. For six months, you do not fly.

The result: the airline decides that it must punish you. You are no longer flying with them. You receive a letter from them stating that you are now demoted to the status of 'normal' passenger.

This is the tyranny of a loyalty programme. The airline's data indicates that you are no longer loyal. The airline must know that you have been a regular, and intense, flyer with them. Rather than punish you, their question should be: 'why is this passenger no longer flying with us?'

The customer is certainly not the centre of this airline's decision-making. Decisions are made according to the rules of the loyalty programme: to retain his or her status the customer must make a given number of flights during 12 months. Decision-making must be concerned not only with the customer history [how much has this customer spent and which products or services have been bought?] but also with customer behaviour [why has this customer stopped flying with us?]. Necessary information on the customer must be captured, and organised, using digital business technologies, so it can be translated into the customer knowledge that can be shared and acted upon.

Fluid, self-organising capabilities — with agreement on the commitment to the customer made at the front line, two essential capabilities must be enacted:

- knowledge that the commitment can be delivered; and
- the business network can be immediately organised to fulfil the commitment.

Traditional organisations will check the requirements against a form of product catalogue. The order desk, the sales person, or account manager will submit the order to the back-office and factory and, in many cases try to escape the consequences of inadequate fulfilment. The mindset that 'once you have sold to the customer, you escape and find the next' must be displaced. The lead person – or *customer leader* –

must have responsibility for fulfilment. This means that he or she must know that the order conforms to capabilities and be able to check the status of fulfilment and be warned on potential, or existing, failure.

The organisation of the fulfilment chain is normally a set of well-defined procedures. Unfortunately in the traditional organisation, one often suffers too little co-ordination or communication between these procedures. When you order the book, who will inform you if it is not in stock? Does the book 'sales person' receive this information? Or do you wait? When the order is complex and many participants are involved in its fulfilment this can be magnified beyond the point of frustration. The business network acts in a totally different manner when digital business technologies enable it. Once the fulfilment requirements are clear, the front line – the customer leader – is able to determine the mix of business network participants required to fulfil the order, to make sure that they are available and can act together to deliver, and then to invoke their activities. The customer leader organises a line – a chain – of fulfilment from those in the business network and mandates them to act.

The customer is now the locus of decision making — decisions are not *made inside-out* – "We will decide what the customer will buy and how the customer will behave." They are made *outside-in* – "We acknowledge the customer requirement. Can we match it and, having matched it, how do we organise to do it?"

2.3   Total Action elements

The Total Action concept will only bring you success if you take account of the name: it demands wholehearted Total commitment, throughout the organisation, and co-ordinated, effective *action* by everyone whose efforts are needed to fulfil a customer's requirement. In a Total Action organisation, that means every single person, because all those inward-facing activities that get in the way of customer focus have been stripped away. Thus, one might cluster the elements that have to be managed under three headings:

– focus on the customer;
– co-ordinate customer information; and
– develop excellence in fulfilment.

Wholeheartedness is the key to successful implementation of Total Action. If you develop customer leaders and a customer action team, but fail to co-ordinate the customer information they need, they can do little to achieve your objectives. Or you might invest millions in the integrated IT systems for the task, and then see it fail because under-motivated, poorly managed people in the organisation don't see the importance of their tasks in meeting customer requirements. Or you get the information and the customer focus right at the sales end, but fall down on fulfilment.

The following sections explore these elements in greater detail, and introduce the tools to implement them.

2.3.1 *Focus on the customer*

This means creating the mechanisms to shift the powerful inertia of a traditional organisation towards paying full attention, respectfully, to the specific needs of a particular individual, or group, who for some reason wants to take up your offer of goods or services. Your organisation's 'listening' is not something to write ads about; it has to be personified, supported, and managed. The key tools to achieve this focus include a person to drive all the behind-the-scenes activities that serve that customer, and a team [temporary or permanent according to the customer's needs] to achieve these activities.

2.3.1.1 The role of the customer leader

The customer leader is the person who makes an organisation's platitudes about customer focus and customer care come true. Consider an imaginary example:

You want a loan. Have you chosen your flights?

You need a short-term loan in order to buy a ticket for a visit to Australia so you telephone your bank. Your Financial Services Manager [FSM] listens to your request. Somewhere else the response might be: 'I will send you an application form; it will be in the post tomorrow.'

In Total Action the response is different. The FSM raises your 'screen' on her 'customer dashboard': her gateway to the bank's information and transaction world. Immediately she sees your customer profile, together with information on your recent transactions with the bank. Meanwhile, you have logged onto your bank's 'Personal Home Page' and you are seeing the information that she chooses to show.

Her first question is: 'Have you organised your travel?' 'Not really.' 'Okay, when do you want to travel, have you any airline preferences?' She has clicked on the travel icon, raising a map of the world. Clicking on Australia she then checks on the date range you have indicated. 'We have some good offers here. You want British Airways for the air smiles. For the price of a normal Business Class return we can get you two Business Class tickets with an overnight stay in Singapore...and a choice of hotels.' She puts the information onto your screen.

You are interested. She is clicking on the travel search icon for flights. 'If we book the tickets from Germany, because the pound is so strong, Deutsche BA has a 10% discount. You'll want a hotel in Sydney?' She sends you the Sydney hotels screen: 'Let me tell you what we could organise. And let's discuss travel insurance.'

You are persuaded. Eventually comes the question, 'About the loan ...?'

That FSM is your customer leader for the bank:

- She is more than a Financial Services Manager although she is the interface to your bank. She is the manager of services that relate to your requirement for finance.

- She is acting on the bank's behalf, using a cluster of organisations with which the bank has established linkages.
- She is the single interface. You don't need to contact other parties unless you want an alternative, comparative source. From the information and transaction centre of her customer dashboard, she is able to organise the entire trip for you.
- She is able to organise a chain of fulfilment. If she offers you flights, hotels, and tickets for the Sydney Opera House, she must deliver them.

For this customer leader, fulfilment is more than ensuring that you have the necessary air tickets and confirmed hotel and other reservations. Fulfilment includes the satisfactory – or delightful – completion of the holiday: combining and delivering the different modules – or service elements – which make up the holiday. In addition, the customer leader must be able to deal with *exceptions* – failures in the delivery of any components and events that may cause the holiday to fail.

For example, when you encounter a problem in Australia you must be able to contact your FSM – by telephone, fax, or e-mail – to resolve it quickly. When your e-mail arrives from the Observatory Hotel in The Rocks in Sydney telling of your mother's heart attack in Kent, whoever receives it at the bank must, immediately, be able to determine your history with the bank and the agreements which have been made; then initiate a new chain of rapid fulfilment, checking travel insurance, booking flights, and doing whatever else is necessary, as quickly and painlessly as possible.

The role of the customer leader lies at the heart of Total Action. The customer leader takes full responsibility for satisfying the customer across the full *customer service cycle*: the full cycle of the relationship with the customer from *seduce* through *fulfil* to *renew*, as shown in figure 2.6. The customer leader is much more than an intelligent sales person – the customer leader must be able to manage and ensure the satisfactory initiation and completion of this cycle.

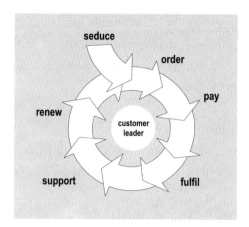

Fig. 2.6.   The customer service cycle

The customer leader may be permanent for a particular customer – as in account management – or temporary for a specific order. The customer leader can be software, rather than a person. For example, Dell Computer's customer leader is an interactive web page. However, in each case the principles of customer leadership are the same – those with temporary or permanent responsibility for the customer have the clearly-defined authority to determine the customer's portfolio solution, invoke fulfilment, and then monitor it.

The customer leader lies at the heart of this cycle:

- from the moment of *seduction* when the [potential] customer contacts the organisation;
- completing the *order* [matching between customer requirement and the portfolio construction which satisfies the requirements];
- *enabling payment* — ensuring that the necessary financial trans- actions take place;
- *invoking and managing fulfilment* — ensuring the delivery of the portfolio solutions;
- *supporting the customer* — managing failure and delivering necessary information so the customer is able to use the solution; and
- *renewing* — developing further business with that customer.

The customer leader cannot act alone. She, he, or it, needs *information support* on the customer, on the portfolio, and on fulfilment, as well as *authority support,* the clearly-defined mandate to do the tasks required. The customer leader must have the following support:

- the ability to access relevant information on the customer;
- the ability to access information on the portfolio of capabilities – the modules of the 'holiday' – which can be combined to create the holiday;
- the ability to guarantee the availability and initiate delivery of the [holiday] modules;
- a system to monitor the fulfilment process [including alert on any failure].

In the vocabulary of Total Action, this customer leader is able to:

- *ensure actions at the point of customer contact* — guiding the customer into a solution which is of value to that customer;
- *organise a portfolio solution* — organising a collection of deliverables from the organisation's portfolio of capabilities which bring value to the customer and build the bank's business;
- *be the locus of customer decision-making* — guiding the customer's decision-making according to his or her requirements while taking and enacting decisions according to the capabilities of the organisation's portfolio and the delivery which can be made;
- *make all activities customer activities* by *managing transaction integration* — linking and organising transactions across the chains of information and events which will lead to the successful visit; and
- *exhibit interactive capabilities* — interacting with the customer and with the internal and external back offices to fulfil the customer's requirements.

This is achieved with the help of two important Total Action components:

- the *customer action team* — the formation of the 'fulfilment team' from the components of the business network available to the customer leader; and
- the *customer dashboard* — the informational electronic window on the customer and the organisation allowing the customer leader and the customer action team to manage the customer interaction and the possibilities for and delivery of the solution.

2.3.1.2 The role of the customer action team

The important characteristic of the customer action team [or CAT] is that it combines the skills to meet the specific goals for a specific customer.

The mandate of the CAT is to drive the organisation so that the customer becomes the centre of the business universe. CAT members derive actions directly from the customer and ensure that the organisation works from the customer into the organisation. This is working outside-in.

The enormous benefit of CATs is that they break through the myopic views of the typical large organisation. In too many organisations the knowledge gained at the customer front is simply not used. Myopic managers don't see their counter personnel as part of a customer team, or as a source of customer intelligence. Shop people are often too busy filling shelves to even note that customers exist; they behave as if they are invisible to the customers.

Working with the customer leader, the CAT must direct the activities of the Total Action organisation and its business partners, supported by instant and accurate information from the customer dashboard and by managing the commitment and fulfilment process for each customer within their temporary supply chains.

The CAT does not fit to the mindset of the typical organisation today but it demands that this mindset be destroyed. It acts as a high-performance customer team. It combines the relevant skills and capabilities to determine and meet the goals of the specific customer. In accord with the concept of 'modularity' each participant in the team, while independent, has to function together with the others as an integrated whole. 'Design rules' are required defining how everyone functions together, how they interact, and their standards of performance. Above all, each participant has to share clearly understood, communicated, and agreed goals: 'What are we going to achieve with this customer?'

To work, the CAT must have:

- clear definition of the capabilities and availability of each member [definition of the portfolio of capabilities];
- clear definition of goals [what is to be achieved with the customer] and role [what and when each participant must fulfil];
- clear communication between each member [the shared vocabulary];
- clear reporting to the customer leader on the status of fulfilment.

The CAT triggers the temporary supply chain to ensure fulfilment. But it must do more. It must take full responsibility for this named customer, not only at the moment of ordering and until delivery, but also in understanding and developing the customer's behaviour. It must mine knowledge out of the various customer encounters. It knows that you are planning to travel alone and that you enjoy opera. As a result, it can trigger behaviour and linked sales to ensure that you remain an ongoing customer.

Like the customer leader, the CAT may take various forms. It may be an ad-hoc, but directed, combination of participants or, as in the case of account management, may have a stable core [the account team]. This permanent team will dwell on the ongoing management of the relationship with the customer augmented by new participants [the 'virtual' account team], depending on the position in the customer service cycle.

There must be no breaks in the chain of command and control which

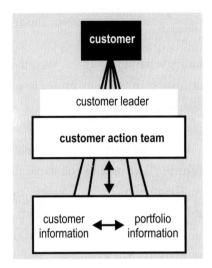

Fig. 2.7. The CAT role

originates from the CAT. It must behave as an entrepreneur within the boundaries of control defined by the organisation. As figure 2.7 shows, the CAT becomes the 'organiser' in the information value cluster. The CAT can serve two roles:

- managing the continuing relationship with a complex customer [particularly in opportunity identification and analysis]; and
- combining to ensure the fulfilment of the agreement with the customer.

In both cases, the basic need is for clear and rapid communication according to a shared vocabulary.

2.3.2   *Co-ordinate customer information*
Access to information is a critical element of Total Action. However, access is not a passive activity, nor is it a technology platform alone. Making the customer the locus of decision-making demands that all information about the customer and the organisation's performance with the customer is immediately accessible and can be acted upon.

Once information can be mobilised, the organisation can be mobilised.

Here the technology and the people come together. Only if the systems are effective, and the people understand how to use them properly to meet clear objectives – taking care of that named customer – will the organisation gain benefit from its investment in the digital business technologies – or, for that matter, from its investment in able people. Behind the scenes, the IT experts are an important part of the drive to achieve Total Action. This is especially crucial when it comes to gathering information about particular customers and their particular requirements, analysing it, and moving it instantly to those who can do something to meet the customer requirements, starting with the customer leader and the customer action team.

The IT department is a key tool to co-ordinate customer information: One product of its involvement would be what we call the *customer dashboard*.

2.3.2.1 The role of the IT department

The lack of mutual understanding between business people and the IT departments of the large organisations has become a serious issue. Board members seldom really understand the complications of the computer, but are painfully aware of their dependence on it. The high priests of corporate IT gradually come under attack: 'What value do you provide to our business?' One story [perhaps apocryphal?] illustrates the lack of mutual understanding:

Why bother?

During a benchmarking visit, a number of senior executives were shown the capabilities of a new airline booking system. It automatically produces a ticket for the passenger, creates the invoice and checks the payments, puts all passengers together, makes a loading plan for the aircraft, produces a crew schedule, and pays the stewardess for overtime. In addition, the

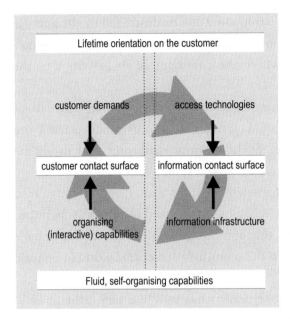

Fig. 2.8. The collisions

airline would know which agent booked this passenger, the passenger's plane, and the name of the stewardess.

'Why would you want to do that?' asked an IT Director.

How do you transform your information systems groups to become a formidable asset in your digital business future?

As figure 2.8 illustrates, collisions between the external and the internal worlds occur at two levels:

- the organisation's ability to match its behaviour and capabilities to the demands of the customer; and
- the organisation's ability to put in place the information infrastructures to interface – seamlessly – with the customer access channel technologies.

Such collisions are by no means new, but the use of digital business technologies certainly show them up. In unresponsive organisations, an intelligent and responsive front-line can be destroyed by the autistic organisation in the back rooms. This is the world where a customer enquiry is not answered, where the customer is an interrupt to the business process.

The IT organisation must become the *digital business competence centre*. IT must deliver a well-defined *service* to its customers across the [internal] customer service cycle. It must interpret and direct its behaviour as the collaborative IT business network.

The IT department together with business management must take control to ensure that these technologies are used collaboratively rather than chaotically. Curiously, this becomes possible because of the chaos of the Internet rather than in the seemingly structured world of historic computer systems.

The transformation of IT departments has proved a very difficult task. Usually it has begun with an in depth analysis of 'all problems at the same time'. The result is often that the internal departments become the 'customers' of IT. Although appealing in its simplicity, the idea of the 'internal customer' is seriously flawed. Internal service contracts can be negotiated but the tools for measuring performance are usually absent and negative figures are too easily hidden. The ability of the internal customer to source elsewhere is, in practice, very limited. If alternative supply is used, the internal customer will be subjected to monstrous treatment on other counts. The protection of an 'internal market' with its artificial prices and the needless bureaucracy would be very different if the IT department were an independent company. Such an approach is similar to outsourcing, but can reduce the company's abilities to gain a strategic foresight on the use of IT.

I'm sorry, it's a problem with the computer

The check-in person is standing in front of a queue of passengers, all trying to make their flights on time after the computer system has crashed. It doesn't help him to send out an IT person to learn about the customers. They both learn more than from the thousand words of the consultants or a bashing by the chief executive – they find out, in no uncertain terms, what customers want.

Another IT professional sat in with the electricity company's customer service agents, facing a queue of irate customer who had received the "red warning" bill threatening to cut off their service [before the first bill had been sent from the giant new computer]. His learning had long term benefits, but he could offer no short-term help.

In a retail outlet, the sales agent is trying to satisfy the string of customers buying the latest 'special' offer, but he has no stock and no means of checking availability. Someone else may call it a 'computer application', but he calls it a headache.

Such real life experiences – the atoms of disservice – ignite new understanding and foster a new understanding by IT of their 'internal customer'. Not only of the managers but, more importantly, of the men and women in the field who meet the real customers on a daily basis.

Subject the IT people to the same stress and frustration as the people in their company who have to work with their IT tools in real life. The goal is to make IT people really understand that they must provide the platform and the IT capabilities for the business to perform! In addition, they must recognise that they, IT professionals, have a responsibility for translating the 'magic' of their technological capabilities into business actions. They must not wait for the business to tell them what to do.

The general issues around engaging the IT department as a key part of Total Action [or as a key element of Fatal Inaction] are discussed in Chapter 3. In terms of co-ordinating customer information, one of the key tasks for the IT department is helping develop the appropriate customer dashboard, to support everyone involved in getting and fulfilling the customer's order.

2.3.2.2 Creating the customer dashboard

The customer dashboard supports the customer leader. Its primary functions are:

- to ensure that the necessary information on the customer and on the portfolio are delivered to the point of need; and
- to provide the customer leader with the ability to invoke and manage the fulfilment process.

Such a customer dashboard, therefore, can take a variety of forms, from a portable computer used by sales people and account managers to the direct support given by the computer and telephone system for telephone banking. In the case of Amazon, selling books over the Internet, the customer dashboard and the customer leader coalesce into the interactive web page used by the book buyer.

The customer dashboard is the information window between the customer and the organisation. It presents the necessary information on the customer, the organisation's capabilities [the portfolio] and the organisation's performance for the customer.

The customer dashboard allows the customer leader to navigate the necessary information on the customer and the portfolio to define and invoke fulfilment of the customer solution. In addition, it can help management look at the organisation's performance for the customer and the customer's contribution to profitability. Thus, it can be:

- a 'customer navigator' providing historic and operational data on the customer;
- a 'performance navigator' providing data on the organisation's performance and the 'performance' with the customer;
- an 'activity navigator' providing detail on the status of activity with any customer;
- a 'portfolio navigator' providing data on the history of and demand for specific 'products' within the organisation's portfolio.

The customer dashboard is not an executive information system: it is a short-term, immediate tool, an operational system to help the CAT members achieve their mission with the customer. This dashboard approach differs also from the control screens of modern automatic call-centre systems. An automatic call distributor [or 'ACD'] registers customer telephone calls and agreements that have been made. It does not delve deep into the operational systems of the organisation and does not try to monitor overall performance. As with many sales activity and account management programmes, ACD's are often restricted to managing only the contact with the customer.

The aircraft control panel

The control panel in a modern aircraft is an impressive 'dashboard'. In real time, all information from the plane's most important functions is fed to the pilot. Engine data, fuel consumption, speed, direction, position, are presented in a simple, meaningful and clearly understandable format. If something is wrong or if the pilot wants to inspect the functioning of a special part of the plane, he can 'drill-down' into the information like someone linking information on the Internet.

In the old days, without the support of this kind of dashboard, the pilot had to determine whether the flaps were still working by looking at them. As aircraft technology advanced, the cockpit gained many different meters, panels, switches and knobs, each with its own function. The pilot could then control the 'factory' remotely without making physical inspections. The meters, panels, switches and knobs were all linked to their own specific functions of the plane but were not integrated. The pilot had no way of taking a rapid overview of the total situation. Motor pressure needed a different meter because it is different from air-inlet pressure. In today's cockpit, the pilot is able to observe:

 – that all planned activities are operating correctly;
 – that internal performance is meeting the requirements of the external environment [like the customer/market];

- navigation data: the route map [like the business plan for the customer] is being followed;
- deviations from the norm and the expected which must be acted upon;
- that the internal activity is responding to new circumstances; and

Technological advances have made it possible to 'integrate' information and control systems in the way which is seen in the modern Boeing 777 or, even more strikingly, in a fighter jet where much faster responses are demanded. Flight plans can be fed into the system by the pilot and air control. At every point in time during the flight, the plane's functions and the route are being monitored: there is *constant measurement of performance to target.*

Digital business technologies make constant measurement of performance to target possible in a business situation. The customer dashboard shows necessary control information from throughout the organisation, presented in an integrated manner according to activities for the individual customer. Its uses include:

- gathering data continuously on how the organisation as a whole performs for specific customers;
- checking and monitoring the data with respect to the agreed – or planned – performance targets for the customer; and
- deciding and co-ordinating, to take corrective or anticipatory action.

The customer dashboard has four components, as shown in figure 2.9. These are usually quite specific to the specific organisation:

- *the personal workbench* — the personal facilities such as electronic diaries, activity planning, word processing, spreadsheets, graphics, e-mail and relationship management.
- *the customer performance plan* — the structured template for the corporate plan with the customer[s]: the customer plan including opportunity plans, campaign plans, and management reports. The

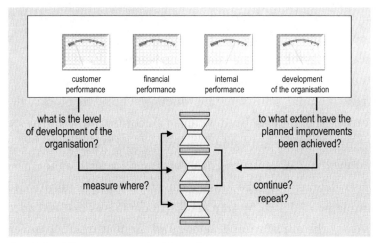

Fig. 2.9. The customer dashboard

performance plans determine which 'meters' are shown on the screen.

– *the service monitor* — the workbench is linked to the fulfilment and support processes of the organisation and has access to the relevant data on individual, operational processes. These tools allow quantitative analyses such as 'investigate' [zooming in or out of databases], 'what-if' analysis, forecasting on trend lines, and measurement on key performance indicators.

– *the communications tools* — the networking facilities connecting to the back office systems and the company internal networks for telephony, e-mail, videoconferencing, and more advanced groupware systems.

The customer dashboard approach has a number of attractions:

– *The most critical customer performance data are being clearly defined as measurable indicators* — the organisation's performance down to the individual customer can be monitored and modified where necessary. The customer leader and the customer action team can determine, in real-time, such data as where the operational problems are, who performs particularly well with the customer, and why. Since a complete log of customer interactions is kept, it offers an invaluable source for integral company planning.

– *Implementation can be incremental* — by making the systems architecture modular, with separate functional building blocks, the customer dashboard can be developed according to prioritised requirements determined by engaging outside-in. There is no need for a total overhaul or replacement of systems. Instead, as the user interface is determined, the ways data are fed to the dashboard can be implemented step-by-step. Links to databases can be added or removed as the application develops and use matures. Moreover, the technology components are generally available and low-risk.

By applying an Intranet approach, a company can ensure that access to customer information drives the organisation. For example:

– *for business and sales planning*, forecast and historic data as well as identification of key customer trends [by customer size or industry sector] can be consolidated immediately for every account, no matter how many;
– *for product planning*, information on customer requirements, performance data on products, and information on competitive activity can be readily consolidated and analysed.

Digital business technologies make it possible to maintain a constant measurement of performance to target. All kinds of control information can be shown in a clear and integrated manner, presented in the context of the individual customer. Metrics on performance *for* and *with* the customer [and customer groups] can be set and measured for service cycle participants.

Using a customer dashboard, the customer leader, as well as management and members of the customer action team, can keep watch on operational factors:

– the status of all planned activities;
– internal performance on all parts of the customer service cycle;
– navigation data, making sure the route map [the business plan for the customer] is being followed;
– deviations from the norm and who is doing what about them;
– alerts...that something is wrong and must be dealt with; and
– that the customer action team is responding as circumstances change.

At a strategic level, the customer dashboard can be used:

– to gather continuous data on how the organisation as a whole performs for specific customers;
– to check and monitor these data with respect to the agreed – or planned – performance targets for the customer; and
– to support decision-making and team co-ordination in order to take corrective or anticipatory action.

The customer dashboard is not the same as the traditional executive information system presenting [often-historical] strategic data on the performance of the various functional units of the business. Though it is also convenient for strategists, the customer dashboard is an operational system to assist the customer action team to achieve their mission with the customer.
The customer dashboard uses digital business technologies to help define, monitor and deliver nearly-complete communication on:

– the customer;
– the portfolio of capabilities;
– the status of fulfilment; and
– the performance metrics of the organisation with the customer.

Organising information: infomediation
When information can be organised and associated in useful ways,

two parties gain new value from it: *those who use the information and those who organise the information.*

We call this ability to associate and organise information *infomediation*. It adds value for these parties but those parties who hold parts of the information may find that their role is diminished.

Business is familiar with *intermediation* in which an organisation adds greater value by placing itself between a supplier and its customers. New entrants in the car insurance industry, for example, give the customer call centre access to information and can search information about many possible insurance providers to produce the 'best deal' for the customer – breaking the traditional bond between insurance company, agent and customer.

Another familiar concept is *disintermediation* in which an organisation bypasses the intermediaries between itself and its customer, to deal direct, as Dell Computer exemplified. Digital business technologies enable many new contenders here. The Internet serves only to increase these capabilities.

I want an air ticket

You wish to fly from Paris to New York. The traditional options have been:

- contact your travel agent. He or she scans the flight databases of a range of airlines to recommend the best deal. However, the choice may be tainted by the commission which he or she receives from specific airlines;
- search the small ads for ticket deals. Call each vendor and make your choice;
- determine which airlines fly between Paris and New York and call them to see what is available.

Rather than 'telephoning' you may find that many of these parties have an Internet presence where you can question them.

Traditionally, flight information is organised by the individual airline and is normally limited to flight times. You rarely find good prices and

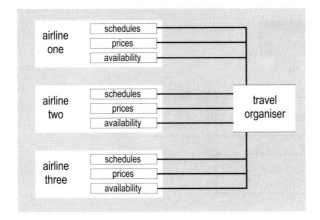

Fig. 2.10.   Infomediary for travellers

flight availability. Organisations – infomediaries – are now on the Internet claiming to determine the best deals for you. Some innovators have gathered world wide flight schedule information so that, by accessing them on the Internet or using a CD-ROM you can find out the flight times for all airlines: 'I want to know all flights between Paris and New York on Thursday the 17th leaving Charles de Gaulle after noon."
American Airlines EasySabre goes a step beyond this. As an Internet subscriber you can determine available flights and prices and make a reservation.

This illustrates the traditional world of 'product catalogues'. We can assume that every airline has three basic databases, as shown in figure 2.10:

– flight schedules: the times of departure and arrival of each of its flights;
– flight pricing: the range of available seat prices for each of the above flights;
– availability: which flights are available at which price.

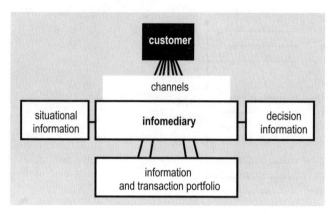

Fig. 2.11. The infomediary value cluster

When a travel organiser – or infomediary – can gain access to and organise these information bases, he or she is in a powerful position, able to determine the optimal flight in terms of price and timing.

The airlines ultimately stand to lose millions of dollars. The airline seat, and information about that seat, has actually become a commodity. While certain passengers will always make full fare, business class reservations, many others will seek these best deals once they are available. Those less traditional passengers might, for example, time their reservations to take advantage of the airline yield management system. The airlines will try to prevent this information escape, in particular protecting information on availability and yield pricing. However, sensible infomediaries can probably gain sufficient information from 'public' or 'subscription' services to make very educated guesses on the possibilities.

The concept of the *smart software agent* adds another layer of concern [for the airlines and the traditional travel organisers] or opportunity [for the passenger and infomediary]. Rather than access the information, the seeker sends this software agent off into the World Wide Web with the question: 'best deal on flight from Paris to New York'. The agent returns with the answer. Such an approach is already being tested in general searches for information on the www or best prices on specific products.

Infomediaries: enablers for digital business — infomediaries organising and managing access and linkages to information are becoming, and will be, prime catalysts in the digital business world. They find, organise and use a value cluster of information sources for their customers, as figure 2.11 illustrates.

An infomediary can take many forms. It may be the web page, as in the Tesco or Dell examples, or the customer leader, as in the travel loan example. The infomediary may be:

- *passive* — simply providing links to further information or other infomediaries [such as a www portal or a telephone enquiry desk]; or
- *active* — able to interact with the customer and enact transactions [the supply chain]. In the vocabulary of Total Action, the customer leader is an *active infomediary*.

The World Wide Web is rapidly developing into a web of active and passive infomediaries. The Tesco and the Amazon web pages act as active infomediaries to their informational and product portfolio. A growing group of infomediaries have developed on the www: the so-called *portals*, or doorways to information. These portals are passive www infomediaries providing value adding by organising the value chain of information to the individual. The portal's only inventory is *knowledge about the location of relevant information* [other infomediaries]. In 1998, portals attracted some 15% of web traffic and 67% of US advertising spend [$870 million][11]. Portals developed from the early search engines to begin to provide a cluster of information value for their users. They can wield substantial power, as the Yahoo example demonstrates.

The Yahoo example[12]

Jerry Yang and David Filo, Stanford University engineering students and 'web surfers' formed Yahoo in 1995. In 1993 they posted their list of favourite sites[13]. In 1995, this list became Yahoo and a nascent search

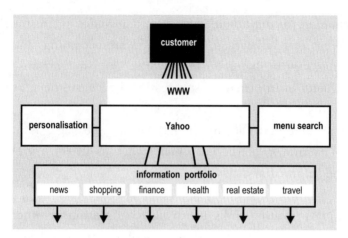

Fig. 2.12. The Yahoo value cluster

engine for the World Wide Web. Yahoo 'went public' on August 25, 1996 with a share price of $97.50, giving a market capitalisation of $9.1 billion. This was 305 times their projected 1998 earnings of 32 cents a share. In 1998, Yahoo's share price rose to 23 times that original 1996 price. In 1998, over 40 million people visited the Yahoo site each month, to navigate their way to places of interest on the web. This compares with the 30 million who tune into NBC's top TV show, 'ER'. Figure 2.12 illustrates this infomediary's use of its value cluster.

The members of Yahoo's information portfolio are themselves active and passive infomediaries.

Those infomediaries that become the portals of preference for individual users are able to control the information and transaction portfolios that they access. Thus they must be as neutral as possible. Many people will, of course, choose to bypass the portals, either going directly to members of their own portfolios, or using a number of portals. If a portal demonstrate its unique value, it can win loyalty, particularly as the portal becomes, like Yahoo, rich in knowledge and easy to use. Intelligent software search agents might replace portals although it seems more likely that these capabilities will be absorbed in the portal itself.

Portals are very attractive to the advertising industry since they become key travel nodes for Web users. They also have an incredible capability for squeezing information out of their users through the power of personalisation. There is no other mass medium that offers suppliers this ability to communicate with individual customers, and pay attention to their responses. The ability to persuade users to provide personal information and preferences, and also to track the electronic trail they leave as they make active choices, allows infomediaries to gather information of great value to advertisers and to the suppliers who are part of their value cluster. Here are the beginnings of *one-to-one marketing*[14].

Painless but powerful customer information

Normally, you log on to the portal at about 8 o'clock in the evening and spend between 30 and 45 minutes online. You always go straight to the share prices, followed by business news. You often visit the sites for books and CDs. Three times a year you engage in intense activity on the travel sites – sometimes spending up to an hour. Every week you check 'What's on in Pittsburgh' and you often look for information on current plays and operas. Recently you have been paying attention to the 'health' pages and sporting activities. Occasionally you look at sites for intelligent computer games or teenage interests. Only last week you were searching for information on college places.

From this, the portal could build a relatively accurate picture of you, the surfer.

- You are an intelligent web user and are selective on what you use it for.
- You want information on shares. You are likely to be an investor with disposable income. You could be navigated to selected web sites which offer you relevant financial services.
- You buy books and CDs on the web but have established a direct relationship with specific cybershops.
- You live in Pittsburgh.
- Your leisure interests include drama and opera.

- You have a teenage child who is about to attend college.
- You are concerned about your health – probably aged between 45 and 50 – and are seeking a 'physical update'.

...without asking for information on your age, your gender, or your financial circumstances.

In this way, the portals have the potential for infomediation. So if you are a supplier, they might intermediate between *your* organisation and its customers. True, not all your customers would shift, but you would not like to lose discerning customers with a relatively high disposable income.

2.3.3   Develop excellence in fulfilment

Business partners who share a relationship among them, which enables them to do business 'fairly easily' become a *business network*, with whatever degree of formality they feel is appropriate. When one of the business partners wants to complete a transaction, the remaining partners can rapidly form the fulfilment chain. Everyone within the network knows what they must do and they act accordingly so the network works to deliver as one whole.

Such business networks have always existed. They exist within organisations, although they are often constrained to rigid relationships, determined by historic procedures. They exist, for example, with a building contractor to whom you trust your domestic comfort when you decide to renovate the bathroom.

The basic business network: the building contractor

The small, but effective, building contractor has a few, if any, employees. He works with a selection of subcontractors: specialists such as bricklayers, plasterers, electricians, plumbers, and decorators. They know one-another, their strengths and weaknesses, what they are good at, and what they cannot do.

When you select a contractor to renovate your bathroom, he lets all his subcontractors know what will be expected of them. He will prepare a specification of works and a rough project plan, after talking to each one about the job. Their communication will be primarily the telephone, supported by paper. Everyone knows the goal and what they must do to achieve it, as well as the order in which activities must be conducted. The bricklayer knows how to lay the ducts so that the plumber can put in the sewage system. The decorator knows that the paint and wallpaper go up after the plasterer's work. The essential processes are defined and agreed between them. Should problems arise, the business network co-ordinator – the building contractor – keeps in touch so that necessary corrective measures can be taken. This is a business network.

Together the members of this network can offer something that no one of them could do individually. You could try to reduce costs by hiring each one separately, but then you would have to plan and co-ordinate their activities, without sufficient information about how they work. All you really want is a new bathroom, on time, at a specified price, without mistakes or too much plaster dust in the house.

This business has relatively low transaction costs 'because they know each other'. They do not only know each other as trustworthy business people and capable professionals, they also understand how one another's processes work and what is needed to co-ordinate these processes.

When the building contractor wins the next contract, he will work in the same way but several of the participants will be different, because the next job has different requirements or some sub-contractors are busy on other projects. The building contractor may not always use the same plumber or the same carpenter. But he will make sure there is always enough business to keep the business partners in his network occupied. Otherwise they may move elsewhere and not be available when he needs them.

This is a co-operation between individual participants with differing capabilities; with the ability to manage and control all the activities of the many different parties to meet one goal.

Digital business technologies help co-ordination within such a business network. The Internet and its progeny facilitate such business networks. In fact, the concept is very simple but its enactment may be difficult. Some know the misery of the building contractor whose business network is collapsing, whose promises are unfilled, whose subcontractors are always elsewhere or unclear about what they must do. Clarity and communication drive digital business networks.

Excellent management of fulfilment of the customer's requirements is achieved by integrating the management of the demand chain. The demand chain is that outside-in 'relay race' of co-ordinated activities triggered by the customer order or requirement. The business network [sometimes referred to as the 'value web'] is the clearly-defined family of fulfilment capabilities available to the organisation. The customer order, through the customer leader and the customer dashboard invokes the managed coupling of these capabilities to realise fulfilment.

2.3.3.1 Managing the demand chain

The supply chain, from raw material through production to customer, was captured in Michael Porter's concept of the 'value chain'[15], which looked at how internal activities should be organised to achieve a desired margin. Porter divided the company into the individual components which make up the internal value chain (figure 2.13); he then high-lighted the opportunities for information technology to change the ways in which the organisation linked its internal chain and was linked to the chains of its suppliers and customers. By identifying the power of information systems to link the different [internal] value chains of supplier to company to customer, Porter reflects the company-centric approach to business optimisation of that time.

This organisational model, alone, is insufficient for today's challenges. Digital business technologies now enable us to pay attention to the information arrow – the two-way flow of vital information across the supply chain and the activation of chain participants from the point

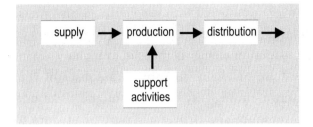

Fig. 2.13. The linear chain of value adding

of customer contact. With interactive capabilities, you can access this information instantly and act upon it. The product arrow is, in effect, reversed since vital information moves 'backwards' across the chain.

The customer as the point of departure. By taking value creation at the customer as the starting point, you trigger the chain of activities for fulfilment. According to Peter Vervest:

> 'You start with the ultimate customer. The value that is created at the point of contact with the customer signals the start of the relay race in the chain. The chain must be linked together rapidly to deliver to the customer within the required service levels, by the required time.'[16]

It takes exceptional management and application of information to achieve this. The chains of activities are linked together rapidly and organised effectively to deliver to that customer according to her or his demands. Anything, which does not contribute to this value, does not contribute to business success. The customer becomes the centre [and the beginning] of the business universe. This replaces the 'pre-Galileo' concept of the organisation and, as a result, the department or business unit at the centre of the business universe.

The customer at the centre of the business universe. In reality we are seeing that companies can now operate in a web of collaborative business relationships and linkages forged with suppliers and customers. According to the modular network design model,[17] the members of the network are all the production elements that are available to form the *demand chain*. The demand chain, in turn, is a subset of this value web, like a line drawn through it, made up of the links and transactions necessary to produce and deliver a service or product to meet a specific customer requirement. In most organisations, these links have been fairly rigid, creating the traditional, fairly fixed, supply chain. Digital business technologies allow you to construct flexible linkages very rapidly, just as the well-organised building contractor can make a single phone call to be sure the bathtub will be installed next Thursday. In Total Action, the organisation seeks to organise the value web on its own terms.

> '*The critical success factor is the speed whereby a company can switch or make links to create value for the customer.*'[18]

2.3.3.2 Designing a modular network

Rapid and effective fulfilment demands new ways of managing the delivery chain. In each interaction between buyer and seller along the chain, there are two over-riding requirements: *unambiguous clarity during the commitment phase* and *orderly and timed execution of the fulfilment phase*.

Unambiguous clarity during the commitment phase

During the commitment phase, an organisation agrees and commits to what it will do for the customer. Every element of the agreement has to be checked, instantly, on 'compliance' with the organisation's capabilities. Commitment depends on *trust* – the belief of both parties that each will actually live up to its promises. Even when you are, like the building contractor, 'only' directing the activities that must take place, you have to ensure that 'it works'. Your back office must function with incredible reliability, since it is no longer acceptable to take the customer order, give it to the order clearing department, and then forget about it. You, personally and corporately, will be to blame for what may go wrong.

It becomes even more important and difficult to ensure trust when links in the chain are to other organisations. When your incoming flight is delayed by Air Traffic Control, you don't usually blame Air Traffic Control. You blame the airline or its staff. From the customer's viewpoint, the fulfilment process is invisible. You only want to see the satisfactory result. Payment implies covenant – an understanding between two parties that agreements will be fulfilled. If you've paid for an airline ticket, you expect to take off, preferably on time. Companies who do not provide what they say are in more peril than ever before.

In the past, companies could satisfy the customer requirement by exact prescription and standardisation of the product or service. In a customised world, where you must make-to-order [as opposed to make-to-stock], all data relevant to the specific customer agreement must be captured before you can fulfil it.

One way to capture order information is computer-based order entry, direct by the customer, sometimes aided by friendly self-service, electronic shopping. However, customisation means more than giving your customer access to an online ordering system through some form of sophisticated product catalogue. You have to be able to handle all kinds of customer initiated requirements which are not part of your standard product catalogue.

Orderly and timed execution of the fulfilment phase

To fulfil a customer's order, you have to gain the agreed collaboration of the various departments of the business network – the organisation and its business partners. As we have seen, significant problems arise when individuals are unable to interact effectively: to communicate, to keep each other informed, to set goals and arrange schedules. Effective interaction has to be created between co-operating members of the supply chain to make it work. This is *integral management of the supply chain*.

The concept of integral supply chain management is simple. You:

- define all activities which must be undertaken;
- find and commit the parties which can undertake these activities within the defined parameters of time, money, etc; and
- manage its sequenced execution.

To achieve this, it may be helpful to use *modular (business) network design*. The key is the ability to determine the *service elements* – those pre-determined components of the portfolio which can be rapidly brought together to become the customer solution – and the ability for *rapid, integrated management of the supply chain*.

Modular (business) network design defines the rules for the selection and interaction of participants in the business network according to the components of the organisation's portfolio which are to be delivered to the customer. The approach is based on the concept of *modularity*. The concept of modularity underpins not just mass production, but also the mass customisation that customers demand today. By building a product out of standardised and compatible modules, manufacturers can not only increase the flexibility of a product family but also organise better for production of these individual modules. Modularity must now underpin service design and fulfilment in the same way that it underpins product design and manufacturing.

Consider the microwave oven. While the top-end model has a digital clock and timer, the lower-end has a coarse knob that can be turned to select different timings. However, the lower end model has a space for the digital timer. Such modularity is inherent into today's computer and car manufacture. It occurs in the same way in the microwave handbook. With the computer and car, buyers can mix available features, or modules, into the specific solution they desire. Such modularity means more. It means that the manufacturers, or assemblers, can divide their processes into separate modules, which can be manufactured in different locations and by different companies, then brought together for final assembly. As a result, they are able to organise their supply chains more effectively. This is the basis for mass customisation. Modularity inflicts a strong discipline on the participants in the supply chain and on the communication and organisation among them:

'Modularity is a strategy for organising complex products and processes efficiently. A modular system is composed of units [or modules] that are designed independently but still function as an integrated whole.'[19]

Such modularity requires rigorous rules of module design and interaction [the *design rules*] that determine the *architecture* of the business network:

- which modules are part of the product and how they function;
- the interfaces: how the modules fit together, connect, and communicate; and
- the production standards: the metrics to ensure that modules conform to the design rules and for comparing their performance.

To design a business network that makes best use of modularity, you follow a logical sequence of steps, illustrated in figure 2.14:

- define your portfolio of products and services as a set of modular capabilities – *service elements* – which can be combined to meet the customer requirements;
- determine how each of these service elements can be delivered: the family of *production elements* which are the activities, or participants, which 'make' the service element [inside or outside of the organisation];
- determine how the business network – the *process module network* – is organised by defining the rules of interaction for all members

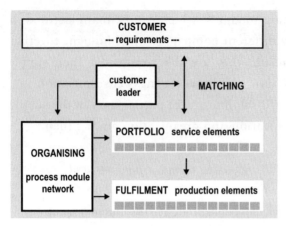

Fig. 2.14. The basics of modular (business) network design[20]

of the business network. This would include the delivery parameters [cost, lead-time, time to complete] so you can calculate the financial and time constraints for delivery;

– ensure direction by the customer leader – the *temporary supply chain co-ordinator* – who triggers and manages the process module network.

When the service and production elements and the process are clearly defined, you can improve the flexibility, speed, quality, and costs of fulfilment dramatically. Once the rules are clearly defined they can be expressed in software. Reconsider the example of Dell Computer. On the web page, or at the customer service desk, the components – or capabilities – of the PC can be selected and instantly communicated to production. In parallel, delivery people can be alerted and prepared to fulfil according to the customer requirements. Should any delay or failure occur in the fulfilment process, Dell's customer leader – the service desk – can be notified immediately or the customer e-mailed directly. In addition, product development planners can have instant information on customer preferences or non-preferences, guiding them toward demand for new services or products.

Membership of the business network can also give you new flexibility. You can add new participants instantly, as long as they can conform

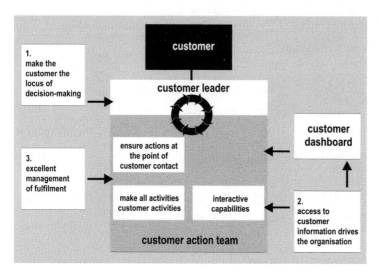

Fig. 2.15.   The Total Action model

to the rules of behaviour of the existing network. Or the flexible business network can adapt its rules according to the new participant.

2.4   The Total Action model

Actions at the customer front demand excellence in fulfilment – the integral management of the supply chain. Modular (business) network design can enable the excellence you need: clear customer commitment and managed flexible working. For a specific customer requirement, the customer leader with appropriate information support tools, is able to configure the requirement from available components [service modules], make sure that they can be delivered within the given time and cost, and activate the chain of supply to deliver the solution. This means transferring the necessary information and instructions, or interacting directly with the fulfilment participants [the production elements] while monitoring progress and being alerted on exceptions. Unless you put this kind of flexibility and decision-making into the hands of people at the customer front, you are likely to expose the Fatal Inaction of your organisation.

The elements of the Total Action model can now be brought together,

and we will explore how they work in real organisations. Figure 2.15
shows the three key steps:

- *make the customer the locus of decision-making* — organise customer
  leaders and customer action teams;
- *ensure access to customer information* — enhance interactive
  capabilities with effective information platforms and customer
  dashboards;
- *manage fulfilment* by *integral management of the demand chain*
  in the organisations *value web* [business network].

A rigorous method of working outside-in to engage the whole organisation
must to be put in place to deliver lasting results.
The objectives of this Total Action approach are to:

- ensure actions at the points of customer contact;
- make all activities customer activities; and
- improve interactive capabilities.

The key elements of the Total Action approach
The key points of Total Action are:

- *Every point of customer contact is a 'moment of truth'* — Digital
  business technologies allow you to be in contact with your customer
  through many channels. They give customers a way to assess the
  performance of your organisation. For Total Action you must put
  the customer first, not only at the front line. The whole organisation
  must act toward the customer; all non-customer specific activities
  must be eliminated.
  Breaking corporate autism is not a trivial task. You must assess to
  what extent internal priorities are set by real customer activities.
  The inner logic of the inward-facing organisation creates powerful

obstacles to change. Digital business technologies offer new ways to find out about customers and create value out of a dynamic web of people and organisations. But you have to change the unresponsive ways in which the large organisation tends to think and function today.

– *Make the customer the locus of decision making* — You have to know exactly where and when your organisation meets the customer. Your front line people must be able to interpret their mission at that very point of impact and be empowered to decide on the best course of action. They must be supported by customer action teams.

– *Enable excellent fulfilment* — once the customer action team has decided on a course of action, its fulfilment must be immaculate. Integral management of the supply chain means streamlining key processes within the organisation as well as in interaction with its business partners. With modular design of the supply chain, you can customise to meet individual customer requirements.

Actions at the points of customer contact and access to information must be fundamental capabilities of the Total Action organisation.

3   Weeding out Fatal Inaction

Fatal Inaction – the antithesis of Total Action – is revealed by failure with the customer. It can be seen in intense activities which have no relationship to an organisation's performance with that customer. Many [if not most] organisations have distanced themselves from the customer. Over time they have fragmented into discrete specialist functions and departments to manage, maintain and develop their operations. These departments develop around themselves highly complex and rigid processes and systems. In due course they begin to perceive themselves as businesses in their own right – an error today's 'business unit' focus simply magnifies.

Such organisations often become dysfunctional. Their people, usually intelligent and competent, have become trapped in corporate autism, a serious handicap inherited from task-oriented, production-line forebears. They become inward-facing internal markets for themselves, with rules and behavioural standards that are far too rigid for the digital business world.

Digital business technologies create complete communication and interactive capabilities that such autistic organisations cannot match. Further, they expose and magnify Fatal Inaction, whether it is endemic to an organisation or merely hidden behind its outmoded behaviour. Fatal Inaction must be identified and weeded out if an organisation is to survive… beginning at the customer front.

3.1   What is Fatal Inaction?

Fatal Inaction is the inability to manage the customer service cycle effectively. It results in a failure in performance. You can invest large sums to put into your front-line, giving your customer ease of access and interaction – yet this excellence is vulnerable, destroyed if your people are unable to fulfil the customer's expectations. In the past fatal inaction could be hidden from the customer; it was commonplace; customers expected broken promises, late deliveries, and wrong orders. Now, the digital business technologies give customers much quicker, broader access to the organisation. Thus, your inability to perform becomes highly visible. Worse yet, competitors are beginning to exploit the technology possibilities and make goods on their promises. Customers notice, and tell each other.

If Fedex continually reported delays or lost packages to its customers, they would go bankrupt. If Amazon, the digital bookstore, failed to deliver its books according to its promises, the word would be out [probably on the Internet].

Until recently most consumers seemed to absorb such failure and considered it to be the norm. Today, those organisations that can harness digital business technologies effectively are helping potential customers become dissatisfied with the status quo of competitors' current performance.

In other words, other people's Fatal Inaction becomes your competitive edge – unless you let your own Fatal Inaction become someone else's competitive edge.

Corporate frogs in hot water

Why doesn't the frog jump out of the pot before it begins to boil? The comfort of the warm water seems to lull the creature, and the change is gradual. So the frog boils. So it is with large organisations!

It has been reported that U.S. corporations lose half their customers every five years[1]. People at the sales front have some awareness of this leakage, but no one else seems to notice, until a large customer suddenly moves away. Worse yet, these organisations don't seem to know why their customers defect, or investigate why they go. It is obvious that they are failing with an astonishing 50% of their customer base – yet they don't really regard the loss as important. The defection of the smaller customer is 'averaged out' of the financial reporting. The leakage goes unnoticed, like the increase in the frog's water temperature, until too late.

Most organisations are at least superficially attentive to customers but, many times, the attention is only at the sales front. Organisations with large, complex customers have harnessed account management. Yet, too often one finds that 'account management' translates into a highly effective front-line [the account team], which finds incredible difficulties in working with the organisation's back office. While the customer is highly visible to the account team, that customer is virtually invisible to the back-office.

Those organisations selling to individual consumers have a strong focus on the customer. They know that customers are becoming stringent in their demands and that their expectations are high and rising. It is seldom only a question of price. Indeed, for many services, price confusion is developing. In financial services or mobile telephones, customers say they can no longer understand and differentiate between the price regimes offered by different suppliers.

Today's buyers are making their decisions much more often according to the services that surround products, such as ease of buying, support, and attentiveness. Call centres have been set up to provide a single point of access for potential customers who want to order, to get information, or to get help. However, these front lines can become a skin around the organisation – soft on the outside, hard on the inside.

Many companies are using digital business technologies, including the Internet, at the front line. This is dangerous unless people at the front are supported by a responsive organisation behind them. This vital

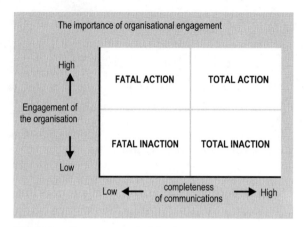

Fig. 3.1. Engagement with the customer

coupling between the front and back offices is critical today. Without it, the responsive front office is powerless since it cannot deliver effectively.

This is our organisational inheritance. The structure and behaviour of most large organisations is governed by what was essential in the past. Bureaucracy is not appropriate to today's business world.

In the digital world it is essential that new ways of engaging your organisation must be determined. If you take no action, total inaction is the ultimate result. The customer increasingly sees the inactivity of the organisation. It is not just that the organisation's fulfilment for the customer fails or that there are no valuable activities with the customer. The totally inactive organisation erects a hard resistance, a skin, between the customer and the sales front. This seems endemic in those organisations who introduce the 'help desk' which appears to have the mission of deflecting customer enquires away from those who are able to satisfy the enquiry. [For many frustrated customers this skin is symbolised, technologically, by the chirpy enquiry system that never gives you an option to speak to a human being.]

A total inaction organisation, recognising its shortcomings, sometimes moves into fatal action: responding energetically, but in the wrong direction. It may not (yet) be fatal for the organisation but can be fatal for the employees who are either removed from the organisation or totally confused and demotivated by the flux of meaningless changes which swirl around them. Change without direction is fatal. All such activity or non-activity derives from the internal, rather than external, focus of many, if not most, organisations.

3.2   The roots of Fatal Inaction

Every organisation has *a compelling inner logic*. This logic determines the behaviour of the organisation and of its employees: the pattern of values, beliefs, and behaviour that are the organisation's essential character. Today it is fashionable to refer to this collection of beliefs, 'the way we do things around here', as the 'corporate culture'. It makes behaviour predictable and controllable; it ensures stability and it ensures the integrity of the organisation.

People have been looking for a 'unified theory of management and organisation' since industrial organisation began. The early writers, notably Fayol[2] and Taylor[3], have had a significant impact on organisational design and behaviour that lasts to this day.

Taylor focused on the worker on the shop floor as a unit of production while Fayol worked from the top of the hierarchy. Fayol, who spent his working life managing a large company [Comentary Collieries], is the father of functionality. In 1916 he identified the key operations of a business – accounting, commercial, financial, security, technical and administration. Administration comprised organising, co-ordinating, commanding, controlling, forecasting and planning.

Over the period from 1920 to 1950 researchers from many organisations and countries propounded coherent families of ideas about people and work. These came to be called *classical management theory* with some basic principles identified by Lussato[4]:

- *scalar concept* — the hierarchical structure with authority handed down from the top to bottom;
- *unity of command* — an individual can receive orders from only one person;
- *unity of direction* — there should be only one head and one plan for a group of activities which contribute to the same objective;
- *exception* — delegation should be optimised with decisions taken at the lowest possible level. Routine tasks performed by subordinates while exceptional tasks should be performed by the immediate superior;
- *span of control* — the optimal number of subordinates;
- *organisational specialisation* — activities should be differentiated according to their objectives, processes, customers, materials, or geographic location;
- *scientific method* — use of experimental methods – observation, hypothesis, experimentation, formulation of quantitative and universal laws, checking and correcting.

Taylor's approach to 'scientific management' was developed in the Midvale Steel Company that he joined in 1878. His objective was to increase production by reducing the range of methods used by different workers to undertake to same jobs. Seeing major possibilities for significant efficiency gains, he targeted:

- *efficiency* by increasing each worker's output;
- *standardisation* of work by dividing tasks into small and clearly-specified sub-tasks; and
- *discipline* through hierarchical authority which could implement management decisions.

In this view of the world, the individual is the unit of production, motivated only by economic rewards. The result:

- tasks and responsibilities are clearly divided between management and workers;
- workers are scientifically selected and trained;
- work is based on rules, laws, and principles which replace ad-hoc methods; and
- co-operation between workers takes place to ensure performance, motivated by economic incentives.

Management managed the work and the workers carried it out according to the dictates of science and the management. Built upon by Taylor's scientific progeny [Gilbreth, Gantt and others[5]], it exists today, particularly in mass production companies.

The classical approach focuses on rules, roles and procedures. It creates bureaucracy, characterised by belief in rules and the legal order[6]. Management and organisational theory and practice have moved forward, generating a plethora of recommendations and advice. We have seen a shift away from the belief in the existence of a universal theory towards the view that we need a diversity of organisation structures.

The increasing turbulence of the environment has forced radical rethinking on how organisations organise. Stability [with brief periods of instability] has been displaced by instability [hopefully with brief periods of stability]. Burns and Stalker[7] proposed the *organic organisation*, flexible and self-regulating to cope with the uncertainty of its environment. Kanter[8] suggested that functionally based – or *segmentalist* – organisations cannot respond effectively to the environment. The division of knowledge into sub-units of an organisation means that it cannot recognise or act on a problem collectively. Organisations that integrate can more easily identify key events. By linking knowledge from different parts of the organisation, small events can be identified as symptoms of larger, more important, events and the organisation can begin to adapt.

These principles complement the Total Action approach. In fact, Total Action enables organic and integrative behaviour, with fluid, self-organising capabilities. While there is a diversity of recommendations from practitioners and theorists on how to design effective, adaptive organisations, the ideas, principles, guidelines and theories don't seem to reduce the complexity of the task. Mechanistic organisations – stable, predictable, automated, and bureaucratic – can no longer survive. Now, the management literature focuses on responsiveness, adaptability and flexibility, with a concomitant deluge of how to manage change. The *need* to change is widely recognised. *Achieving* that change is a challenge few organisations really meet.

Today's complex organisations can seem self-correcting, returning to their old stability. The compelling inner logic of organisations tends to resist pressures for change. For most large organisations, this logic can be traced directly back to Fayol and Taylor, although it may conflict with an organisation's self-perception. This anti-change logic is rooted in the inability to manage complexity without the tools for interactive capability discussed in chapter 2. To understand how the internal logic translated itself into the autocracy of the internal market and corporate autism, we must return to the roots of business.

Back to the roots of business

The small company has its simple and compelling logic: find a customer, satisfy the customer, keep the customer, make a profit. The relationship between customer satisfaction, profitability and growth is clear to everyone. When the customers are satisfied, they remain. When they are dissatisfied, they walk away and the business begins to fail. Professor Theodore Levitt gave a fundamental business invariant:

> 'The purpose of business is to create and keep a customer. Creating
> a customer means doing those things which will make people or

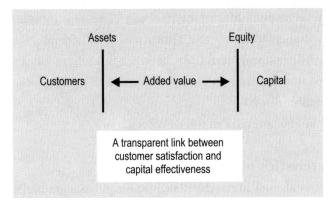

Fig. 3.2. The simple logic of the small company

companies want to do business with your company rather than with your competitor [or do no business at all]."[9]

To achieve this fundamental purpose, every activity within the organisation must be directed at creating and satisfying that customer, to ensure that he or she continues to do business with you.

The small company acts as a true organisation: a social arrangement for the controlled performance of collective goals[10]. As individuals its members are unable to achieve the goals which they believe are worthwhile. Collectively, the organisation can achieve them. Large or small, it must organise its scarce resources, which means that the performance of the individual, the department, and the whole organisation must be measured against well-defined metrics. Performance must be controlled:

- defining metrics;
- measuring performance against them;
- determining whether performance is satisfactory; and
- correcting deviations from the norms.

Membership of the organisation must be controlled. Inability to perform to standard means loss of membership. Members must comply with the mandates of those responsible for controlling. The requirement for controlled performance leads to the allocation of functions, the division of responsibilities and activities between members of the organisation who group according to shared activities. The emphasis is on *performance* and *control* .

It is at this point that the internal market evolves.

3.3   The characteristics of Fatal Inaction

That internal market is almost inevitable, because employees gradually get their recognition, their rewards, their advancement, and their development – all the things that motivate them – from internal sources. Some of the greatest frustrations for employees come when they can see and feel what the customer wants [after all, most of us are customers ourselves in out outside lives], yet they know that filling that customer need would actually flag them as 'disloyal' or less than trustworthy to insiders.

As organisations grow, we see a number of effects of this internal market, that inevitably hasten the death of the organisation – its Fatal Inaction. These include:

- the comfort factor;
- inward-facing leadership;
- measures unrelated to the customer;
- internal competition;
- corporate autism; and
- hardening of the IT arteries.

3.3.1   *The comfort of the internal market*

As it grows, the small organisation tends to develop activities which are important to managing the organisation but seem to be of no importance to winning and maintaining customer business. The larger the organisation is, the more activities are developed that have lost the vital link to winning and maintaining customer business. In some companies the value of those internal transactions far exceeds those with customers. They develop an internal market characterised by internal financial transactions, taking place between internal suppliers and internal customers. More invoices flow internally than externally and the only customers are internal customers.

Organisational inertia develops, built upon the logic of the past: 'We do things this way. This is our style and culture. It has worked in the past. It works now. It will work in the future! We must ensure that our customers conform to our behaviour'.

The internal market confuses and destroys the clear relationship between customer satisfaction and capital effectiveness. This internal market draws heavily on the company's resources and intelligence, replacing customer time by internal time. The invariant is broken. They have lost the fundamental purpose – to create and keep a customer. For the majority of workers the Levitt invariant is displaced by the new inward-facing logic which is characterised by the mandate of 'Make your budget'. This budget, an internal artefact, rapidly becomes distant from the basic reality of the balance sheet.

Internal competition drives departments to design their operations according to their own criteria and objectives. Functional excellence invades the reward system, with each top manager [or baron] holding the mandate for a specific function: administration, distribution, finance, legal, manufacturing, marketing, sales, and so on. No one owns the customer process; therefore it diminishes and dies.

Traditional organisations operate on the model: managers think, workers do. Many managers believe that their role is to ensure that their staff does what they are supposed to do. They 'administer, maintain, organise, plan and schedule' using internal financial measurements to ensure that the business is 'under control' in the immediate future and that 'there is a future in the business'.

All the managers are usually capable, intelligent and well trained, dedicated to what they feel is right for their organisation. Individually they are very competent; collectively they are not! The organisation does not function as it ought. These organisations talk of change but everywhere there is the comfort with, or insistence on, sameness. There is a love of routine and procedure that breeds a strong resistance to change. Change awakes fear. External – customer, market, and competition – stimuli are rarely felt beyond the sales front. But the corporate memory is strong and numbers, often the wrong numbers, are recorded and remembered. Can such an organisation be spontaneous or innovative?

It is easy to find internal reasons or scapegoats: failing leadership, poor communications, and incorrect organisational structure. While these can contribute to these difficulties, our experiences show that these are not the true problem. After all they can be changed. They are, in fact, a result of a rigorous inner logic that has become so strong, so overwhelming, that a good reason can always be given to explain why the organisation acts as it does and why it must not change. This is not a matter of culture. Culture concerns the behaviour which individuals develop as a result of the compelling inner logic of the organisation that has been developed long ago. This logic determines the reasoning of decision-making individuals and the way in which they behave. As a result, it can restrict the effective performance of the organisation. Get this logic into focus and it can be made visible and addressed. Change this logic and you can improve performance!

3.3.2   *The boss leads, the customer bleeds*

Managers believe that they must maintain and strengthen the strict inner logic, since they know it will secure their future careers. The competent manager is forced to pursue internal goals that are increasingly remote from the customer. Such a manager cannot make career-limiting decisions.

This appears to happen no matter how useful the work. In the same school as Parkinson's Law[11] – 'Work expands to fill the time available for its completion.' – the Peter Principle[12] tells us that managers tend to rise to their level of incompetence and sit there, like the skin on sour milk, preventing any other movement. [One management guru told an audience that Peter had confided the proof of his principle was the number of middle managers who believed it.]

Even today, such cynical assessments of management continue. Adams in 'The Dilbert Principle' argues:

'The most ineffective workers are systematically moved to the place where they can do the least damage: management. This has not proved to be the winning strategy that you might think.'[13]

While light-hearted, such remarks create resonance for many people. As individuals, they can see failure with the customer. They can see what can and what must be done. But they are powerless to break through the invisible tyranny of the inward-facing organisation.

3.3.3   The wrong metrics

Inward-facing business metrics do not relate to the true metrics of business. People have to spend their time talking *about* the customer rather than *with* the customer. Customer dissatisfaction and defection go unnoticed while performance and opportunity gaps increase. Depart–mental performance is measured on 'meeting the budget' and 'delivery to the internal customer'. Managers are accountable for meeting financial targets that they themselves have defined and which have been merged into the corporate business plan [with the usual adjustments]. Should they fail against these targets, it is always a result of events outside their control. Such reasons include the failure of other business units to perform as promised, or the unexpected behaviour of the competition, the distributor or the customer. And, within the complexity of the internal market, no one is able to challenge this logic.

The company's internal market inflates the status of the internal customer above that of the real customer. The behaviour of this internal supplier is coupled tightly to these internal customers. This dependence on the internal customer helps breed a culture of disrespect for the unseen external customer. With the internal customer's dependency embedded in the logic of the business – 'They can't survive without us' –the internal supplier can allow its performance and delivery to sink gradually below the norms the internal customer finds acceptable. This internal interdependence is a compromise that has satisfied the internal business criteria of the two units to ensure their mutual survival: *'We will both do what we have to do to ensure that our boss is satisfied.'* Informal rules and personal relationships overcome any attempts to achieve formal, rigorous measures of performance. As long as everyone operates within the boundaries defined by job descriptions and hierarchical position, business life feels comfortable and individual careers blossom. People do not like to be measured. When performance measures are applied they try to adjust the system to meet their own survival criteria and enhance their own rewards.

3.3.4 The customer is an interrupt to the business process

Too many organisations force the customer to behave ac-cording to their own rules. There are product managers with one primary goal: to ensure 'shelf-space' for their product. This aim conforms to their goal of ensuring profitability, or possibly only turnover, for their product family. They need no real comprehension of the customer's requirement for a 'solution'. The customer exists to meet the product manager's budget objectives. Should the real requirement be better satisfied by another product within the company's portfolio – a competitive internal product – the customer may be actively discouraged because the sale would contribute to another business unit's success.

As a result we find companies with parallel channels to the same market or customer. Each channel is sustained by the ambitions of product or business unit management – and each adds to customer confusion. A manager in a large Japanese company said he was visited in the previous twelve months by over 20 different sales people from the same supplier, each touting a different optimal solution. This fragmentation of the company's image becomes the breaking-off point for many customers. Life is even more difficult for the potential customer who must wade through product information organised according to the internal structures of the supplier, rather than the potential requirements, or questions, of the customer. The customer must meet the internal standards and procedures defined by the seller: 'This is the way we do it – take it or leave it.' The customer's specific requirements and standards are not considered. This is usually understood particularly well by the sales person who can conform only to the dictates of the back office. The self-absorbed organisation imposes its operating practices, standards and constraints on the customer. The real dependencies are reversed. This has been acceptable in the comfortable markets of the past when customers were not in control and had to take whatever could be supplied.

The situation has now changed. It is no longer 'caveat emptor', but 'caveat vendor'! Customers now demand that you conform to their requirements. In a competitive marketplace they can make relentless demands on price, quality and service. Above all, there is a market democracy – intensifying competition – that allows the customer to be promiscuous in a market of over-supply.

At the end of the day, the original logic of business still remains – as the customers walk away, the shareholders and the banks become dissatisfied. Then the crisis begins.

The over-riding result of the inward-facing logic is that the organisation is:

- characterised by internal mechanisms that prevail over the demands of the external real market;
- sustained by the processes of forced internal trade, which determine the standards to which the external customer must adhere;

– producing work which absorbs the corporate resource, so reducing
the capital effectiveness and potential of the organisation.

Catalogue Solutions: the wrong metrics

Catalogue Solutions is a successful mail order business. However, business
is not increasing, and management is concerned:

- revenues are flattening: the number of orders is increasing but people
  are spending less in total;
- the telephone order desk is at capacity and is increasingly unable to
  deal with customer orders; and
- delivery is becoming a problem: unfulfilled orders increasingly cause
  problems with customers.

Collectively, and individually, management is addressing these concerns –
which they interpret as the need to increase revenue with their customers,
increasing sales activity and, where possible, reducing the headcount.

The logic of *Catalogue Solutions'* business is straightforward: deliver
catalogues; take orders; deliver goods; and receive payments.

The company has three main business units: Catalogues, Telesales and
Delivery Systems. These fit the logic of the business. In other words:
Catalogues sells, Telesales takes the customer orders and Delivery delivers
the goods.

Marketing suggests that customers should be offered more to buy, but
the Catalogue business unit manager points out that since the catalogue
is only published twice a year it will take eight months before the change
has any effect. Incorporating new products will increase the costs of
producing the catalogue. Besides, there are delivery problems with the
current range.

The Telesales business unit manager suggests that Telesales must either
increase the number of tele-order staff or open a new centre. If the new
centre is in some remote, job-starved part of the country the new staff
can be paid at much lower rates. In parallel, why not hand over all the
delivery logistics to one of the many, highly reputable and effective delivery
companies which keep on sending their account managers to glorify their

capabilities? The manager of the Delivery business unit disagrees: 'Delivery is a critical competence and we must do it ourselves. It is just getting more difficult.'

The metric: the rule of 52. The key metric for the call centre is the number of orders per unit of time: the 'rule of 52'. Operating throughout the day and into the evening, the 3000 call centre people must take the customer's order as quickly as possible...then move on to the next order. The rule of 52 dictates that customer's order must be taken in 52 seconds. The Telesales staff have had extensive training in managing the order transaction in this time. Support technologies – the automated back-office – have been put in place to ensure that the order is captured and processed and that the necessary logistic and financial activities take place. These support technologies can also monitor staff to measure and report the average time for each order. Those who fail receive further training or leave.

The impeccable and historic logic of *Catalogue Solutions* has taken control. Management argues that the real problem is the recession and the cost of over-staffing. The 'cure': since revenues are flattening, introduce the 'rule of 45' and reduce the telephone order staff accordingly. This is a temporary fix, of course. The organisational change programme, which will be introduced over the next three months together with the new 'customer-in-front' programme, will solve revenue problems. In addition the 'Telesales system task force' will recommend ways to speed up the ordering processes to extract money from the customers faster. Things are looking better.

The front-line people are working to the mandates of the 'rule of 52'. They continually report difficulties in dealing with their customers. Within the time they are finding it difficult to confirm that goods being ordered are really in stock. They also know that when the requested goods are not available they have no time to develop alternative suggestions. They are unable to handle financial questions. The Payment Department must do this – 'I'll try and transfer you'.

Changes are difficult. Handling changes in a customer's order is a nightmare: 'Why don't you place a new order and return the other order when it arrives' they tell the customer knowing that finance will turn pear-shaped as they try to link returned orders, new orders and payments. Even worse, the customer is ordering from the out-of-date catalogue and the prices are wrong. Within the 52 seconds an average of 30 seconds is spent on handling changes, moving complaints and trying to organise the relationship with the back office.

Management acknowledges that the customer order desk is 'the critical point of contact with the customer'. Yet, in reality, it is nothing more than a point of ordering which is beginning to accumulate the signals of failure – the declining growth in revenue.

The key question has not been addressed: how to increase turnover. *Catalogue Solutions* is not badly organised. Individual managers understand how their business has been working and therefore what they must do to improve. Initiatives are in place to solve the problems. The potential of technology, the information revolution, is being mastered so that today's services can be delivered more efficiently. Despite this, most managers know that the situation can be, or must be, improved dramatically. Yet nothing really happens.

This is Fatal Inaction. The customer order desk is forced to act as a hard skin between the organisation and its customers. Above all, the customer is not seen except as an 'address', an 'order' and a 'payment'. The goal is to satisfy the time targets rather than to satisfy the customer. The metrics are wrong: 'complete the order' rather than 'sell more'. Those at the customer surface know this and, probably, the majority of management knows. However, they are trapped in their business logic of the past.

Many of the symptoms of Fatal Inaction are present in this example. It is clear that the organisation has no co-ordinated management of the customer service cycle.

- *no customer leader* — the customer is invisible to all except the 'orderer' on the front-line. We cannot call the orderer an Order Leader since he or she has no knowledge or control of what happens to the order once it is thrown into the back-office systems [except for the customer complaints];
- *no interactive capabilities* — the fragmentation of the organisation into business units limits any ability for order co-ordination, let alone the ability to capture and communicate customer goals [which are probably unknown to the order desk];
- *incomplete communication* — the customer is seen as a collection of orders, probably with no historical analysis.

Curiously, the Amazon model applies directly to this organisation. Amazon and its contemporaries have replaced 'mail order' and 'tele-sales' with 'web interaction'. Look at your primary points of customer contact. They may be people in retail stores. They may be account managers. How do you enable them to become customer leaders?

High Street Electronics: the wrong metrics

High Street Electronics, a large, international, consumer electronic company asked the following question: 'we have given our sales people intensive training in effectiveness. We have re-organised the store layouts. We have given them a computer system that allows direct access to product data. Yet we have seen no real performance improvements. Why?' The company had satisfied what it felt were the basic criteria for improving sales effectiveness:

- they had consulted staff;
- they had organised the stores for ease of customer access;
- they had trained staff in effective sales techniques, including understanding of the company's mission statement;
- they had placed digital business technologies tools at their people's fingertips.

Yet the company was not succeeding.

We asked managers why they weren't successful. They could not give honest answers; they could only respond by protecting their positions. We asked the sales staff. They had to live with the problems. But they said no one listened to them. They wanted management to understand the real issues at the sales front. Could we help?

The top managers were persuaded to spend a few days in selected stores talking with the sales staff and working beside them, to gain some first-hand understanding of the issues. As a result, the real concern began to emerge: *the customer encounter was failing.*

As in *Catalogue Solutions*, the impeccable logic of the company was dictating that the task of the sales person was to *fulfil the order.* Strictly stated: 'Ask the customer for the order number, nothing more!' Sales-performance effectiveness was being measured in terms of 'sales transactions', in response to management demands that specific products be pushed at one time or another.

If the customer was uncertain: 'I'm not sure about the features, but I know the kind of price I want to pay and the basic functions I want', the sales person would rapidly guide the customer to the 'shift it' product of the week. The next step was to persuade the customer to buy the company's service/guarantee contract [which sales people felt offered little more than the law demanded for free, but generated plenty of profit for the company].

Worse yet, the 'rule of 60' came into play: 'Don't spend more than 60 seconds with the customer unless they are going to buy something!' If they want information point them at the brochures. Then, when they return, develop the selling situation.

The sales people had a dim view on the fancy computer support: 'It's been built for order taking – handling the transactions. It's got nothing to do with the information I need to do my job!" Consumer electronics can be complex in terms of variety, price, and functionality and like all products they have a variety of descriptions which can be translated into customer benefits –but it requires time and effort to make the translation.

Notice the invisibility of the customer. These discussions are centring on *internal mechanisms* [the rule of 52, or the rule of 60]. They consider change programmes which will not address 'the customer', but just re-organise internal behaviour according to internal efficiencies. Are they re-organising the deck chairs on the *Titanic*? Company-centric behaviour is a characteristic strengthened by internal market behaviour. The authors liken it to the behaviour exhibited in autism[14].

3.3.5   Corporate autism

The authors use the term 'autism' with care. It is a serious disability which can be managed in the human condition. We chose it to reflect the behaviour of many organisations who are in Fatal Inaction with their customers. They exhibit many similar symptoms:

- self-absorption, which is detached from outer realities;
- indifference to external stimuli, which are ignored until they become painful;
- obsessive insistence on sameness – routine procedures – with a strong resistance to change;
- little spontaneity; and
- an excellent memory for specifics such as numbers or tunes.

Chip of genius or ship of fools?

In his book 'The Man Who Mistook His Wife for a Hat', Oliver Sacks[15] described the behaviour of twins who, unaided and without difficulty, were able to exchange increasingly large prime numbers, a feat which is impossible for most people. He observed their behaviour as each spoke a large number, followed by an even larger number from the other twin. Their behaviour was incomprehensible. It obviously gave the children great satisfaction, yet despite a basic, recognisable pattern, it had no meaning to the observer. After analysis, the truth and complexity of their numbers and the genius of their behaviour was determined.

The twins had a 'chip of genius' which was of great importance and entertainment to themselves, but for the outside world had little relevance except as an example of autistic behaviour. Can a large organisation behave in the same way? Hide a chip of genius by behaviour that has meaning only for itself. Become self-absorbed? Become a ship of fools? Most organisations begin with a chip of genius that differentiates them from the existing world and forms the basis of their success growth. Many, though, seem to lose the basic roots of business.

Previously, we posed the question: 'How do you know that people in your organisation are undertaking activities of value to your customers?' Try this analysis in your own organisation. First, estimate the balance between internal and external activities. Then choose a cross-section of managers and actually measure how they spend their time, according to the following categories:

- *internal* — activities related only to the internal organisation such as planning, budgeting, control, etc.
- *external* — activities concerning – or visible to – the outside world [regardless of whether the outside world takes an interest in these activities]. The external measure was concerned not only for the customer, but also for activities such as market research and analysis, advertising, etc.

Most people expect to find a ratio of about 40% internal to 60% external activity in a commercial company, with a higher internal focus in non-commercial organisations, particularly government. However, when they actually take measurements, they consistently find the ratio more than reversed: in most organisations 80% of activities are internally focused [with 20% devoted to the outside world]. More alarmingly, we consistently find that:

- this ratio remains almost the same for both commercial and non-commercial organisations; and

– the activity emphasis on the inside world grows, sometimes rising over 95%, the higher up the organisation you look.

There are notable exceptions; some CEO's may spend over half their time with customers. Perhaps your own research will reveal such exceptions. At the sales front you naturally find more time spent on external customer activity. But look further and you often see that much of this time is really to meet internal requirements. Some senior account managers spend 80% of their time trying to manage their own organisations, not as customer leaders, but as project managers.

Some think it is appropriate for top management to concentrate on the internal operations and direction of the business. We often find such managers devoting nearly 100% of their time – and overtime – to internal affairs, filling their diaries with internal meetings for three months in advance. Does all this internal time really help achieve success with customers?

3.3.6   Hardening of the IT arteries

The effects of the internal market are most visible when you consider the IT department of a large organisation. And, tragically [because the change is so difficult in a functional IT culture that has surrounded itself with technological cotton wool], it is precisely that IT organisation that must become an integral part of the strategic team that brings new life into an organisation with Total Action.

Some IT professionals have made the transition to management thinking, and can operate at board level, often in the guise of Chief Information Officer. For others, though, the symbols of membership in their profession actually distance them from awareness of the world it should be serving. These IT leaders find themselves in increasing conflict with their organisations. Their systems, as they grew better and cheaper, demand less mumbo jumbo and more realistic use.

Digital business technologies can emphasise and expose the organisational inadequacies in Fatal Inaction organisations. Core **in**competencies rise to the surface. Digital business technologies simply help the customer discover them sooner.

The high priests of IT

As technology started to make, seemingly, dramatic leaps forward, corporate leaders were trying to align their IT departments to their own business needs. It was becoming very clear that the emerging digital business technologies would have a deep impact on how they ran their businesses.

The tyranny of business units

A European airline was addressing the challenge of revitalising the IT department and bringing it closer to the needs of its customers, both internal and external.

There was a clear vision: They needed effective application of information and telecommunications technologies to help fend off increasing competition in their marketplace. They needed to improve service delivery to their customers, determine new, effective internal and externally linked processes, and take unnecessary cost and activity out of the organisation. Management understood the need for information architectures built on telecommunications and computing infrastructures. They were committed to the concept of the 'enterprise superhighway' that would link information, applications, and people across the organisation, and bring them closer to customers and suppliers.

The project began to flounder on the functional splits between the different business units and functional departments delivering IT, telecommunications, and end-user applications. Two issues applied the brakes to the airline's ambitions. First, the responsibility for the cost and ownership of the information infrastructure [the 'enterprise superhighway']; and second electronic mail and messaging.

Each business unit had its own cost and profit responsibilities and, over time, had evolved its own, sometimes effective, IT capabilities. Despite significant efforts for corporate co-ordination [centralisation] of a shared information infrastructure, the compelling logic of past behaviour was overwhelming. In addition, the question of 'standards' was writ large. Each business unit had evolved its own standards along with individual IT solutions. The firm had more than 15 incompatible e-mail systems! Under the imperative of sharing information and providing access to all that needed it, the central IT organisation was mandated to propose and realise both the e-mail and enterprise superhighway solutions.

Logic both compelled and divided. Those business units who were well down the line of realising their own business unit superhighways demanded that their own e-mail solution become the norm. Business pressures meant that they could not afford to wait for the enterprise solution to be studied and delivered. Every time the central organisation proposed an approach, it was rejected. Units said, of course, that the central organisation was far too slow to recommend and implement what was needed. In addition, cost allocation became an over-riding issue and disagreement continued on how it should be done and who should pay for what.

The organisation faced a fairly common impasse. While the technology platforms were available and the intent was clear, the behaviour and objectives of the individual participants continued to keep them apart. There could be only one real route out of this – a dramatic shock, which would create clear understanding and agreement throughout this organisation.

IT is as important as finance, but it does not have the same status. It is difficult to imagine any meeting of the board without 'finance' on the agenda. This is not true of 'information': in many organisations the information director is not even a member of the board. It is easy to lay the blame for this at IT's office doorway: 'They don't understand me and I don't understand them'. This is now unacceptable.

We now have an intense need for mutual understanding. Otherwise, quite simply, a business will fail. The goal of the business executive need not be to master the digital business technologies – but you have to understand what you can do with them. On the other hand, the goal of the IT executive *must* now be to master the business. Perhaps the IT leader needs to spend a week at the sharp end, fairly regularly, to see what really happens.

The tyranny of the status quo

The IT professional. An IT professional for a major airline was asked how he saw his role in delivering to the – virtually unknown – customer. He responded: 'I receive the specification. It tells me what I must do, how long it should take and what money should be spent. I do it and if I'm lucky, if there are no interruptions, I deliver to that specification.' We asked: 'Do you have any influence on what can be done to improve the specification?' 'Of course', he replied, 'but I'm not tasked to do that. Besides there is no time and who would listen?'

The marketing director. The marketing director addressed 25 IT professionals who wanted to understand the airline's customers. Claiming to have little knowledge of the magic of IT, the marketing director asked for their views on the Internet. What did they think of it and why it might be important?

Their responses centred on TCP/IP and new technological developments which they had heard of like JAVA, the magic of accessing databases anywhere in the world, and how the Internet could be a wonderful solution to the company's e-mail enigma of over 15 incompatible corporate systems. The director asked further: 'Which of you is using the Internet?' From the 25, three said they had experience of it, at home. There was a rumour that some in the organisation were 'studying it', but they had never met these people. When asked what it meant for their business, the room went quiet.

I want to seduce my customers. The marketing director told them about his recent visit to the USA, and some opinions he was beginning to form on what Internet might mean: 'It is a tool for seducing customers and learning much more about them!' he said. 'What I think we need is a web page. To start I would like our frequent flyers – our card holders –

to visit the page. I want to find out more about them. For example, I would like to know about their children. If my preferred customer, the frequent flyer, has a nine-year old daughter, I would like to know her birthday. Then, one to two months before, I would like to offer this frequent flyer a package to take the daughter and the rest of the family to Disneyworld.'

'However, I would like this at the beginning of next month or, even better, next Tuesday. I don't want to wait while you study the technologies and the possibilities, generate a report and proposals and then argue about how it will be implemented. This business is moving far too fast for us to wait'. He paused for a moment: 'If you guys can't do it, I'm sure that we can find someone who can!'

This discussion should not have had to take place. IT professionals must take on the role of *translating IT capabilities into business deliverables*. They should scan the possibilities of the technological horizons to find business advantages. This misalignment between business and IT leads to serious business disfunctionality: IT becomes disconnected from the true business imperatives and from the real customers of the business. The end result is inevitably fatal inaction. When access and interaction begin, this organisational alignment connection is vital. New IT capabilities should not follow organisational capabilities, they must lead one-another. Remove the endless discussions and arguments concerning ownership and responsibilities and the continuing misery of centralisation versus decentralisation. The IT business discussions must not centre on the technology of the infrastructure, or the incredible difficulties of connecting A to B.

It seems to be a contradiction that those responsible for delivering the new digital capabilities act as if they themselves can be locked in a museum of learned behaviour. One can see:

- inherent distrust of the IT department by business managers;
- ongoing complaints on the performance of IT;

– fighting between IT and business management over responsibilities, costs, failure to fulfil, or lack of understanding;
– IT people with little or no understanding of what, collectively, they are delivering to their internal – and external –customers;
– multiple, different, incompatible solutions being delivered in different parts of the organisation.

3.4   Moving out of Fatal Inaction

An organisation in Fatal Inaction is a terrible sight, like a person who has been diagnosed with a life-threatening disease. In the same way, to achieve any chance of survival, the organisation has to recognise the severity of its condition, accept the diagnosis, and then marshall its resources to fight for its life.

As people who have fought cancer show us, it *can* be done – but it isn't easy. Are there steps that can help an organisation move out of Fatal Inaction, or better yet, avoid it in the first place? Wholehearted commitment must be at the root of every change. The entire organisation needs to be engaged if it is to survive and grow towards Total Action. The steps towards survival include:

– customer-centred leadership
– customer-centred metrics
– customer-centred management and planning
– customer-centred IT
– customer-centred change.

3.4.1   Customer-centred leadership

The command and control ethic of 'managers think, workers do' must replaced by a complete, unified and pervasive focus on the customer throughout the organisation. Everyone needs a clear view on how to deliver value to that individual customer: to deliver excellence in every aspect of winning and continuing business with the customer. Many managers recognise the overhead of meaningless activity. Yet, they assume that this must be the status quo – the way things are. Breaking the tyranny of this status quo is non-trivial. Removing non-customer relevant activities can unleash new energy in any organisation. This energy can then concentrate on achieving profitable success with customers. The chain of satisfaction and fulfilment is delicate and subject to breakage. Where this chain is broken, or never really existed, you find a mix of internal mechanisms, autistic behaviour and invisible customers. The central theme of Fatal Inaction is that *inadequate performance* stems from the *wrong performance metrics*. *'Managers think, workers do'*. Control has been a central theme of scientific management. Taylor asserted:

> 'An absolute necessity for adequate management is the dictation to the worker of the precise manner in which work is to be performed. Management can be only a limited and frustrated undertaking so long as it leaves to any worker any decision about the work.'[16]

Contrast the Taylor view of management's role with the widely repeated 1953 quote from Konesuke Matsushita, founder of the Japanese empire:

> 'We in the East are going to win, and you in the West are going to lose. There is nothing that you can do about it. Your problem is in your head. Your companies are built on the idea that the bosses think, the workers do. You think the essence of management is to get the ideas out of your head into the hands of the workers. We in the East know this is wrong. Entrepreneurship is far too complicated, far too risky to be left to the brains of a few at the top. We know that management is about mobilising every ounce of intelligence that the organisation has.'[17]

3.4.2   Customer-centred metrics

Select any of your employees and ask a simple question: 'what did you do for the customer today?' An employee actively engaged with a customer project may give very clear answers. They become nebulous when you ask the next question: 'What did your boss do for the customer today?' Customer-based performance metrics are absent in most large organisations today. You may find 'Customer Charters' or 'Customer Value Statements' but rarely are such statements translated into operational activities; instead, as Foy points out[18], they simply increase the dangers of cynicism and hypocrisy.

Performance metrics that are truly customer centred are more powerful than the standard 'customer satisfaction' metrics that organisations usually define for themselves. Those normally assess customer satisfaction with respect to specific attributes of the organisation's performance, seldom assessing how the organisation really meets customer goals. In addition, they tend to operate on variances with industry norms – *best in class*. While the 'satisfaction metrics' can be useful, true customer-centric metrics concentrate on the continual measurement of performance towards the customer and high-value business for the organisation.

Customer-centred measures ask tough questions:

- Where does this customer want to be, and how well are we helping?
- Where do we want to be with this customer and how well are we getting there?
- How well are our processes performing to achieve these goals?

Customer-centric performance metrics – like fulfilment – must be communicated across the demand chain, because they are an integral part of the objectives. They are also an integral part of modular (business) network design. The definition of the *process module network* contains generic metrics, including the fulfilment parameters for the participating *production elements*. Individual customer metrics are embedded in specific plans for the customer. An account plan, for example, contains agreed parameters of fulfilment for the specific customer. In Total Action such metrics are fundamental to *interactive capabilities*.

3.4.3   Customer-centred management and planning

Classical account management gives us a template for Total Action, as figure 3.3 shows. The account manager is permanent customer leader, while his or her account team acts as the customer action team. For specific situations in the customer service cycle [opportunity analysis, bid management, fulfilment], the account manager draws on resources from inside or outside the organisation to form a temporary virtual account team – an extended customer action team.

As customer leader, the account manager takes full responsibility for the customer, including:

- gathering and analysing information on the whole customer and the customer's situation [business environment, customer service cycle];
- developing and implementing the business plan for the customer supported by the full customer action team;
- monitoring and reporting on the performance of the account manager's organisation *for* the customer;
- managing the full service cycle for the customer by managing and directing all activities according to the goals defined with the customer and the commercial agreements between them.

In reality, few account managers are true customer leaders. While they have responsibility [and accountability] for the customer and the organisation's performance for the customer, they rarely have the authority or mandate to achieve this. Hence we see the too common breakdown between goals and activity on the front-line and lack of response in the back-office and factory.

The conflict between account and product management

This breakdown occurs when a previously functional or product-oriented organisation installs account management as the managed interface between the organisation and the customer. The existing channels of

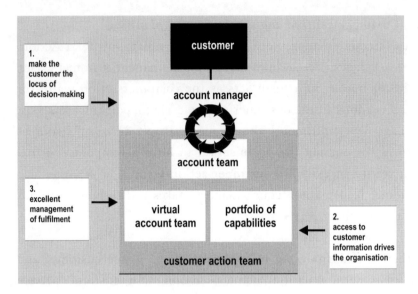

Fig. 3.3. The template for classical account management

communication within the organisation [which would be managed by the product house and the sales force] must adapt to the new interface. Product management sees the advent of account management as a threat, rather than an opportunity, since this intervenes in their relationship with the customer. The performance metrics for product management usually centre on:

– turnover and profit per product line;
– accumulated turnover and profit for the product house;

both according to pre-agreed budgets. In addition, product-performance and delivery-performance metrics are often defined and agreed with the customer:

– the product accords to agreed performance standards; and
– the product house delivers according to agreed metrics.

In many cases, product management and account management act according to differing goals and therefore differing performance criteria. This becomes very visible when the organisation has a portfolio where products are combined to produce customer solutions and/or when one product can be substituted for another.

The account manager's objective is to organise the company's whole portfolio to bring value to the customer and to the supplier. The product manager's objective is to organise his or her product lines to bring these values. The sales force objective is to organise a selected family of products [sometimes the whole portfolio] to selected customers. Both the product manager and a sales person may have a number of different buyers in the same account. As figure 3.4 shows, the account manager regards the account as the sum of a marketplace of buyers.

Within this situation it is difficult to align the account's goals with the different goals of supplier representatives interfacing with each 'customer' in the account. This means that integrated, customer-centric performance metrics are difficult to define and apply. Such organisations are exhibiting the kind of Fatal Inaction the catalogue solutions company suffered [see Chapter 3.3.4]:

- there are few, if any, *interactive capabilities*; and
- there is *incomplete communication* within the organisation regarding the customer and his needs.

The account team may have near-complete communication but cannot transfer their knowledge into their own organisation. The account manager has difficulty accessing information held within the sales force or product departments.

Towards Total Action: the key role of the account plan
The need is for a consistent and accessible information base on the account so that, indeed, access to customer information can drive the organisation. This is the role of the *account plan*, as shown in figure 3.5.

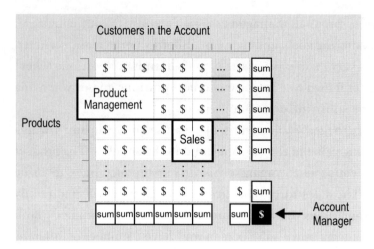

Fig. 3.4. Diverse responsibilities

Often, the account plan is regarded as a static paper document, constructed by the account manager once a year to satisfy the performance metric of 'producing an account plan'. Once created, it can then be shelved and accessed occasionally, say when the next year's account plan is about to be reviewed by management. In some companies the account plan never reaches the eyes of product managers, unless they are drawn into a specific customer opportunity or project.

The account plan should be central to the customer, product, sales, and business planning. It is not a 'document'; it should be *an interactive (electronic) information base* detailing the organisation's relationship with the customer and the specific business plan for that customer's account. As figure 3.6 shows, in a well-structured electronic form the account plan can be a shared information and planning resource for the whole organisation. It can be a foundation for developing interactive capabilities so the information is presented in the most appropriate form for the different members of the organisation's business network. Thus customer information is a collective asset shared and augmented by everyone in an organisation. The tools for such *customer dashboards* are gradually becoming available. The customer dashboard approach can be applied in virtually any circumstance to clarify and display

Fig. 3.5.   Framework for an account plan

measures and status, as the Fedex example below illustrates. Fedex people today can see information down to each package delivered or picked up.

Fedex: clarity on customer metrics

Fedex's initial approach to performance measurement was to concentrate on the percentage of on-time deliveries, with attention on internal operational metrics. Fedex recognised that customer satisfaction would centre on the number of failures, rather than the numbers of successes; a success rate of 99.5% meant some 1.5 million failures! Furthermore, customers cared about the 'quality' of failure. A lost package was far more important than one that arrived five minutes late.

Fedex developed a Service Quality Index based on 12 kinds of failure and their relative importance to the customer. The importance was ranked on a scale of 1 - 10. For example, a lost or damaged package or a missed pickup would cost 10 'failure points' while a late delivery on the promised day, or an incorrect invoice would cost one failure point. The rating changed for specific services: for example on the highest priority service,

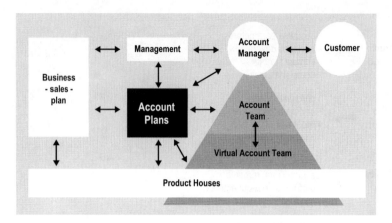

Fig. 3.6. The focal information role of the account plan

a package arriving five minutes late is a 10-point failure.

These simple performance metrics are derived directly from the company's mission statement and translated into performance metrics throughout the organisation.

Without digital business technologies, these performance objectives would be impossible to measure. As a result of its tracking and tracing system [COSMOS] Fedex is able to measure service quality precisely. Every transaction is measured in real time and appears on COSMOS (an open customer dashboard), to inform management, customer leaders, and, of course, the customer.

Fedex uses technology to help its customers track a particular package in transit. Through digital business technologies Fedex makes its performance with each of its customers extremely clear. As we already noted, giving customers access through digital business technologies rapidly exposes any Fatal Inaction in a supplier. Fedex is very clear on its performance metrics.

Clear metrics on performance for the customer and the ability for instant access to these metrics are fundamental to Total Action. Approaches like ISO 9000 and TQM can go part of the way but they tend to freeze the existing activities and processes without improving response to the customer.

The determination of customer-centric performance metrics can be achieved by two of the Total Action approaches:

- *engaging outside-in* — The *opening the eyes* exercise focuses deep attention on current, desired, and mandatory performance. The customer helps define performance criteria and drive them into the organisation;
- *integral management of the supply chain* through an approach like *modular (business) network design* mandates definition of service elements, their associated production elements and the service metrics which the production elements must deliver [the process module network].

How you use these approaches depends on the portfolio, the customer's decision making/buying process, and the fulfilment process, as figure 3.7 illustrates.

You need the modular network design approach whenever there is complexity in the fulfilment process. You need to keep the emphasis away from internal metrics and focus instead on measuring excellence in fulfilment. Although a product may be straightforward [a book, on-time delivery of a package], its fulfilment can be complex.

Complexity in portfolio demands that information on the portfolio and the portfolio choices be organised to be not only available but also valuable to the customer leader and the customer. This demands rigorous service element analysis so the customer leader can configure customer solutions. With a complex customer and complexity in the portfolio, your virtual account teams need both engaging outside-in and the modular (business) network design approach. However, since account management and account teams are people intense, outside-in engagement should be the first step.

Translation into scientific methods is neither straightforward nor

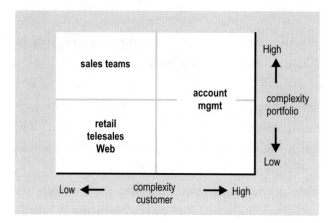

Fig. 3.7. Customer leadership according to the portfolio and customer

desirable. The critical factors for success will lie in the organisation's ability to engage its personnel and quickly determine new or improved fulfilment capabilities.

3.4.4   Customer-centred IT

To secure the digital future of their companies, IT professionals must sort out their operations with unparalleled immediacy and dramatically improve the managerial skills of their departments. IT capabilities are fundamental to Total Action. It can never work if the IT professionals do not understand it. They must build on their technological capabilities to deliver to the needs of the business network.

Meet your internal customer

In one of Europe's largest organisations, we subjected all the IT managers to a rigorous process of 'adopting a customer' – an internal customer. In small teams, they lived with the internal department. With the help of a relatively simple scorecard, the host department managers scored the performance of the IT department from their 'customer' viewpoints. The IT managers then gathered the financial figures and key performance indicators IT used to measure how well it served this internal customer. Together, the host and IT managers compared their measures and perceptions, against the agreed service levels and against the best in their market. This benchmarking had remarkable effects on the IT managers' attitudes.

Since most IT organisations seem to be in a constant state of crisis, we had expected that they would use 'business-is-too-busy-as-usual' as an excuse for not participating. But these IT managers developed a zeal and keenness – they wanted to be involved. Subsequently, multi-level teams from the different IT disciplines came together with representatives of their internal customers and were confronted with the need for:

1. renewal of their relationship with the internal customer;
2. drastic reduction of costs, together with a new understanding of their value;
3. agreeing new performance criteria and measurement methods;
4. new standards of behaviour; and
5. development of new customer skills.

These managed confrontations with internal customers improved the perceptions of the IT experts about the real needs of their customer departments. They also helped clarify the real IT support an operational manager needs, to win with an external customer. As a commercial manager said to his IT colleague:

> 'I do not want to know how big the system is, how many trans-
> actions per second are possible, nor how fast the communications
> lines are! I want to know who my customers are, what they are
> spending, what they have bought, and what they will be buying.'

3.4.5   Customer-centred change

In Total Action people grow accustomed to recognising deficiencies in the customer service cycle and putting in place the small or large improvements to correct them. Management can have an almost infinite capacity for supporting change 'in principle' yet ensure that it does not affect them. The trigger to move out of Fatal Inaction is normally external. Internal change is slow in most organisations, unless everyone perceives impending crisis. For the fatally inactive organisation, internal change is too often 're-arranging the desk chairs on the *Titanic'*. Change is rarely straight-forward. It tends to be untidy. Improvements in one part of an organisation can create discomfort in other parts. People seek the old stability, and so the rigid and compelling logic of the organisation will try to absorb and resist the change. Only the logic of the customer can defeat the inward-facing logic – this is not easy nor comfortable. Customer-centred change can bring positive results when organisations focus, sensibly, on re-engineering [or de-engineering and re-configuring] critical customer processes. When people, individually and collectively, are confronted by a shared, common focus of activity, when their options are dramatically reduced, that's when they mobilise. The authors have found that this is exquisitely true in large organisations. An enemy is required. People need to perceive an enemy that will destroy the comfortable status quo, which endangers themselves. Some will try to escape from the situation [the corporate boat people]; some will seek leaders to whom they can make their life commitment. Others will appoint themselves as leaders to ensure the survival of the organisation.

The true change leader recognises the need for change and mobilises the vectors of change before they are essential. He or she has seen the true shape of the future and is driven to act on it. The authors have met and worked with these individuals. Many have been older senior managers and, in some cases, board members, who can smell the odour of impending doom. Specific examples have been the PTTs, which grew out of traditional government departments with monopoly responsibility for delivering telephone service. As deregulation became possible, then reality, many PTTs have undergone profound changes towards customer awareness as they recognised the substantial impact of future competition. They understand how customer dissatisfaction results in total crisis:

– customers are dissatisfied and choose alternatives;
– competitors take the business;
– valued employees leave the organisation;
– bankers withdraw; shareholders withdraw and salaries cannot be
  paid.

Once you reach the final stage, it is far too late. The trick is to instil
the necessary sense of intense urgency into the organisation at the
beginning – the status quo: customers are merely dissatisfied. This is
what we mean by *engaging outside-in*. Start with the customer and
drive the customer's pain into the organisation. Two questions must
be addressed:

– what is the process of engaging outside-in; and
– what are the organisational factors to be addressed.

We have already looked at the main activities of engaging outside-in.
At this stage we must address the 'organisational factors'. If one aspect
of the organisation is changed it can bring about unanticipated and
negative changes in other aspects. In other words, don't change one
variable unless you are doing it intentionally to trigger managed change
in the others.

3.4.6   *The 4Ps of Total Action performance*
We distinguish four key organisational factors as shown in figure 3.8:
people, process, platforms, portfolio. These '4Ps' must be managed to
act together to ensure excellence to the all points of customer contact –
wherever or whenever the customer encounters, or access, the
organisation.

– *people* — those at the point of contact and those who must support
  the point of contact.
– *processes* — the ways in which people and organisational systems

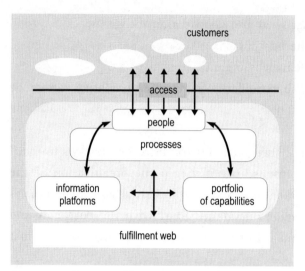

Fig. 3.8. The 4Ps of (customer) performance

act and are therefore co-ordinated and mandated to deliver to the point of contact and derive knowledge from that contact.

– *information platforms* — the infrastructures across which the necessary information is gathered, managed, and provided to the person at the point of contact, the relevant members of the organisation, the customer, and external suppliers.

– *portfolio* — the combination of products, services and capabilities by which the organisation delivers value to the customer.

Two examples illustrate their meaning:

The 4Ps: the gasman cometh

Your gas cooker isn't working properly. With some difficulty, you extract an 'appointment' for the service engineer to come Wednesday morning. You cancel several other appointments and wait through the day but the engineer never appears. Eventually you seek the help of the customer service desk [those helpful call centres]. The help-desk person wasn't very helpful – confirming that the visit was scheduled but having no further information. No reason can be given for the non-visit. However, the supervisor will be informed.

Wednesday evening you receive two telephone calls [during dinner, of course]. Internal communication has taken place! The first was from service engineering to apologise for what had not happened and agreeing a new appointment for Thursday [morning or afternoon?]. The second call came from the customer service supervisor apologising for what had not happened and agreeing a new appointment for the next day [morning or afternoon?].

You stay home Thursday, but still no visit! So the cycle begins again. However you take the trouble to ask the reason for the failure. The Wednesday failure was explained by 'running out of time', Thursday by 'traffic jams'. On Friday the engineer finally arrived and, in ten minutes, put the cooker back into working order.

What is important in this case, apart from your intense frustration, is that the customer service desk had no real communication with the service engineer. It is not beyond the bounds of reason to suggest that a service engineer knows that a visit will not take place or that it will be delayed, and is able [using some form of simple messaging] to inform the customer service desk or the customer.

Why is this important? It is not only that the customer is intensely frustrated and dissatisfied but also that the organisation is incurring significant costs through the mismanagement of scarce resources. The 4Ps help us understand the situation:

- *people* are unable to organise to provide the service which is important to the customer. Perhaps the customer service desk is in place only to deal with billing enquiries and 'standard complaints'. It doesn't seem to be there to answer the diverse important-to-the-customer questions that arise. Furthermore, service engineer scheduling [and fulfilment] is probably the total responsibility of service engineering which is not easily accessible by the customer service desk. We are looking at a 'functional' organisation;

– *processes* have not been determined, nor put in place, to meet specific customer requirements. If they are in place they are not made visible to the customer nor the service desk. Activities are not worked outside-in from the encounter. There is no real process thinking to deliver a positive customer outcome;

– the *portfolio* of capabilities is not being delivered. Rather a catalogue of products is being delivered. Maintenance, requiring the visit of the service engineer, is a product which we have paid for, yet the company does not have the capability to deliver it according to our, the customer's, metrics;

– information *platforms* are not being used to ensure that necessary information is with the person serving the customer. The information certainly exists somewhere but it is neither captured nor communicated. This is a major failing in most organisations. They do not know the information required nor where to find it, probably because they have not asked the right questions.

It doesn't have to be that way:

The 4Ps: Deutsche Bundesbahn

Contrast the gasman's customer experience, with an example we saw on a German train from Cologne to Amsterdam. The conductor brought a very agitated passenger to the headwaiter in the restaurant car. This Brazilian passenger spoke very little English, the conductor spoke less, but the headwaiter was fluent. It turned out that the passenger had left a backpack in a compartment when changing trains at Cologne. Of course, it contained passport, money, a camera and the other essentials of the tourist.

The usual reaction might be to give the passenger the telephone number of the lost property office [hopefully a number that put him in contact with an English, or better, a Brazilian speaker]. However the headwaiter and conductor showed a totally different reaction.

The waiter interviewed the passenger to determine the previous train and, as closely as possible, where the bag had been left on the train. The conductor then radioed the other train and directed them to the bag, which was found. The passenger's face lit up! They then determined the next station where both trains stopped, so the first train could leave the bag for collection. When the bag was returned to him, the passenger was not only satisfied, but delighted and amazed. And a large number of passengers in the restaurant car looked at Deutsche Bundesbahn with new eyes!

In this case the differences are:

– *people* responded effectively to the situation, probably working beyond their mandates. They found the essential information from the passenger and then applied it to provide the solution;
– *processes* were managed to deal with this situation. Taking what was available and organising to fulfil the customer requirement [put me and my bag together];
– the organisation's *portfolio* of capabilities was demonstrated. The solution certainly did not lie in the domain of products which they provide [the 'solving' product would be the lost property service which would not solve the problem]. Capabilities were been mobilised;
– available information *platforms* were used to communicate with the parties who were able assist in delivering the solution.

One of the great failings of many change initiatives is a lack of attention on the relationship and dependencies between these 4Ps. Too many times, there can be attention on one, or two, of these them. This results in short term non-sustainable goals when neglect of the others has produced unexpected negative results. For example, consider at some account managers who have been on a course to explore customer concepts and their application. When they return to the office they find that:

- the information they need is not readily available [where is the data on my customer's revenue and profit history?];
- they cannot connect effectively with their 'factory'. The processes are not in place [I need to bring product management into my account team and they don't know who I am nor what I should do!];
- they cannot translate the portfolio into customer solutions [the portfolio is ill-defined and not accessible in a useful form].

When a change takes place in one or more elements, it tends to cause conflict and pain among other elements. Such friction will always exist, but it can be managed!

3.5   The Total Action scorecard

The practice of Total Action focuses on performance results, in the short term. It aims to reduce the amount of time and resource wasted in internal non-customer related activities. At the same time it increases the ability to communicate and get more value at every point of customer contact. To assess Total Action you have to identify and root out the Fatal Inaction hampering a company. The customer sees this inaction only too plainly – but it is seldom so clearly visible inside the organisation. Two questions are paramount in assessing the need for the Total Action approach:

- *corporate autism* — to what extent are customer activities leading the internal agenda?
- *interactive capabilities* — how well are interactive capabilities developed to support complete communications and instant information access?

The first is a question of present processes and style: the behaviour and culture of the organisation, which are reflected in Fatal Inaction. Can there be a quantitative measure of autism or inaction? Earlier in this chapter, we discussed analysing the time records of key people in the organisation to determine their inside-outside orientation. This is a simple mechanism but, in itself, does not reveal the true degree of corporate autism or identify steps to remove it.

It is more difficult to measure corporate autism. You need a qualitative view on the real nature of the communications patterns both within the organisation and with its customers and business partners. Such measurements would be time consuming and, in fact, distract people from the goal of removing autism. A key parameter is the strength of the internal perception that 'there are customers, they have a choice, and this choice does really influence us!'

The second question is more technical: which communications platforms are in place, to what extent can information be exchanged, and does this influence co-operative goal setting? Unfortunately, technology-equipped organisations do not necessarily perform well with the customer. The relationship between interactive capabilities and customer performance is not straightforward. Some organisations with sophisticated technology are unable to apply it to improve performance, while other companies with a good sense of the collective customer can also do well, sometimes better, without a full command of the new digital business technologies.

The real questions

The real questions must focus on the organisation's current performance with and for the customer. As a senior manager you must ask:

- Is my organisation's current performance adequate? Do knowledge of the customer and customer activities lead our agenda and our behaviour with the customer?
- Is this knowledge communicated, made available and acted upon? Do we support complete communications and instant access to information?

The Total Action scorecard

The customer agenda: to what extent are customer activities leading the internal agenda?

1. Most of my time is spent on customer issues.
2. I know what the customer requires.
3. I understand what we can do for this customer.
4. I understand what we plan to do for this customer.
5. I know who within our organisation takes prime responsibility for this customer.
6. I know my role and contribution to satisfying the customer.
7. We deliver good value for the customer, much better than our competitors.
8. The customer believes that we deliver good value.
9. My manager believes that we receive good value from this customer.
10. I do not undertake activities that are not of value to the customer.

Score each question on a scale of 1 to 5.
1=strongly disagree; 2=disagree; 3=neutral; 4=agree; 5=totally agree.

Interactive capabilities: how well do they support complete communications and instant access to information?

1. We know everything we need to know about this customer.

2. We have accurate data on our performance with this customer.

3. Information on the customer is always up to date and complete.

4. I can easily access the information that we hold on this customer.

5. I can easily access the people within the organisation responsible for this customer.

6. The customer can always contact us.

7. We know about all contacts that the customer has with us.

8. We analyse customer information regularly as the basis of improving our services.

9. All departments as well as our business partners have access to the same information on this customer.

10. Our management tries to give everyone instant access to the customer information which is relevant to them.

Scoring your organisation

Most organisations need to move to Total Action. The approach of *engaging outside-in* determines a measurement of current performance for the customer. This initial measurement can give the present score – a Total Action score –or the present success rate of the organisation according to a number of measurement criteria for each individual customer or group of customers.

A standard procedure for measuring this score is difficult to determine. Measurement criteria are sometimes highly quantified – such as turnover per customer, margin, speed or cost of service provisioning, portfolio spread, share of customer budget. Less quantifiable, but as valid, are future potential, opportunity cost, competitive position, strategic value, etc.

To use the *Total Action scorecard* ask a number of representative customers to name those people in your organisation who are directly or indirectly involved in serving them. Then plot the wider chain of people and functions that are involved in the customer service cycle for each customer.

Ask all those identified to answer the questions on the two cards, and score their answers 1 to 5 [1 = strongly disagree; 2 = disagree; 3 = neutral; 4 = agree; 5 = totally agree]. These scores can then be analysed, particularly with respect to the respondent's own function.

3.6   The sum is greater than the parts

The Total Action approach centres on:

- Re-direction to the customer as the locus of decision making;
- Organise – instant – access to customer information;
- Enable the – integral – management of the supply (or: demand) chain.

These approaches can have differing priorities and need not be undertaken simultaneously. However, it is important to understand that the behavioural aspects of interfacing with the customer and the informational support must be improved in balance. For instance, it does not help to form customer action teams without adequate information on customer performance and the tools to communicate and share this information. Without these, the customer teams cannot act with real customer-centred performance goals. The result can be a lot of training and discussion with no lasting performance results.

The golden rule is to rediscover the customer. Starting from the customer and led by senior executives, the customer action team must gain a deep understanding of the customer and the interactive behaviour of the organisation with respect to the customer.

Critical points are:

- through *customer audits* and *customer focus groups* translate the customer requirements into the performance customers demand of the organisation. Score current performance and measure the gaps between that and the requirement. In addition, you have to evaluate and improve the channels and points of interaction between the organisation and the customers.
- *mobilise the vision and mission for the customer action team and its individual members.* The customer leader and the members of the customer action team must have the deep understanding of this vision – What is important in my business? And their personal mission – What is my role in the business?
- *drive the commitment to the customer deep into the organisation.* Make the customer – and winning with the customer – of prime importance in real organisational life. Ensure that each senior manager and all groups in the back-office 'adopt a customer' and develop understanding of how they must act to 'win in the world of this customer'.
- *mandate the customer action teams.* Form company-wide customer action teams [multi-level and multi-disciplinary]. Ensure that these teams are empowered and clearly mandated for performance

improvement with the customer. This means that the team leaders and members must identify and act on the qualitative improvements essential for this achievement.

– *organise – instant – access to customer information*. Empower the customer action teams by instant communications with the customer and within the organisation. This approach centres on the customer dashboard that provides integral access to customer data as well as supporting the business workflow within the organisation.

4   The Total Action casebook

In Total Action your organisation's performance and decision-making are centred on the customer: the central point or locus of decision-making. Your organisation acts faster and more effectively than any competitor at every point of customer contact. Your customer leaders understand and interpret the organisation's goals – the vision and mission – for each customer. They manage each customer's service cycle, supported by a team of well-informed, highly skilled people – the customer action team. This team has a deep understanding of the customer's requirements, and complete communication, at any time and at any point of contact. The organisation's fulfilment of the customer's needs is effective, responsive and flexible because it has achieved integral management of the demand chain. The organisation becomes fluid and self-organising since it has high interactive capabilities and near-complete communication, as the result of the effective application of digital business technologies.

4.1   The casebook approach

The fatally inactive organisation is readily recognisable, in its failure to perform for the customer and for itself.

How do you recognise Total Action? You feel surprised and delighted when you encounter excellence in an organisation, not only in the quality of its customer interaction but also in its ability to fulfil your expectations. Like a well-designed ship, the fine performance is also aesthetically pleasing. You are surprised that the organisation stands out in how it deals with you, and delighted that it actually delivers what you want.

In the previous chapters, we have explored a number of examples of organisations that demonstrate important attributes of Total Action. These organisations are moving towards Total Action:

- making the customer the locus of decision-making;
- ensuring access to customer information;
- integral management of the demand chain.

To accomplish this, you have to engage outside-in, and harness the capabilities of digital business technologies for external and internal productivity.

In this chapter, our casebook, we have chosen six organisations which are reaching for Total Action. They may not yet have achieved that state but they demonstrate the basic principles. From differing starting points and for different reasons the organisations in these cases have striven to:

- ensure actions at the points of customer contact;
- make all activities customer activities; and
- improve interactive capabilities.

The authors have encountered many organisations who have recognised impending Fatal Inaction, and have set themselves the goal of achieving Total Action. Most have not reached this goal. However, in striving for it they have undergone fundamental changes in mindset and behaviour – particularly with respect to the customer and how they serve the customer. Within these cases, our goal is to illustrate Total Action in more depth and to indicate those steps that can be taken quickly to begin the routes to Total Action. Three of the cases are drawn the 'outside world'. Organisations which each of us can view and respect. We have translated what they have achieved into attributes of Total Action:

- *the US military case* — a non-typical case, where customers may mean 'enemies'. By taking the soldier as the locus of decision-making the reader will recognise what must be done to avoid Fatal Inaction;
- *the American Airlines case* — the, perhaps well-known, case looked at through the eyes of Total Action to indicate the strength of managing and creating access to information;
- *the First Direct case* — the UK bank which seems truly customer responsive and, in effect combined the concepts of customer leader with digital business technologies to redefine the levels of service and the capabilities of retail banking.

The remaining three cases are composite pictures, drawn from the authors' direct experiences.

- *Total Action policing* — discovering and acting on the identity and requirements of the citizen. This case is drawn primarily from experiences with the Police Department of Rotterdam, supported by discussions in other European police forces.
- *Trying to connect to you* — moving from government monopoly to commercial reality as competition hits the, previously secure, telecommunications world. To 'protect the innocent' this case is an amalgam of a number of European telecommunication operators. However two of them – KPN Telecom of the Netherlands and Swisscom – deserve specific mention as 'achievers' in the Total Action model.
- *The postman never rings twice* — creating the customer leaders and customer dashboard to master the largest customers. This case is drawn mainly from experience in PTT Post Netherlands (now TPG) with elements from other postal organisations.

4.2   The US Army case[1]

The 1991 Gulf War showed the pervasive impact of technologies on modern warfare. A member of the Senate Armed Services committee asked the witness how the war was won in 100 hours. Major General Barry McCaffrey, commander of the 24th Infantry Division, replied: 'This war didn't take 100 hours to win, it took 15 years'.

The victory demonstrated rapid mobilisation of skills and resources to deal with the unforeseen, a mobilisation which was possible only through the use of digital business technologies. During the 100 hours more combat power was moved faster and further than ever before in history. The logistic requirements to support a force of tens of thousands of soldiers required 500 ships, 9,000 aircraft, 125,000 vehicles, 1.8 million tons of cargo with 3,568 convoys of supply trucks traversing 2,746 miles of road.

The Gulfwar showed that the US military had undergone a major transition. Traditionally it had been a rigidly hierarchical organisation with sixteen functional 'chimneys' – artillery, aviation, infantry, logistics and so on – each with its own cultural characteristics. It was transformed into a fluid, self-organising culture based on inter-linking three core disciplines: soldier, war fighting capability, and logistics.

The identification of the army's 'customer' might be difficult. But, as General Gordon Sullivan, Chief of Staff, observed:

> 'We've even begun to describe our enemies as "customers" – obviously, we deliver a rather unusual product!'[2]

4.2.1   The soldier as the locus of decision-making

The *digital battlefield* connects all fighting units together in an information and communications network from the field soldier to the commander in chief, thus making it possible for every point of possible leverage in army resources to be obtained.

With digital business technologies, the soldier's position is known electronically and instantaneously. The soldier focuses on a target with a laser, using a fingertip cursor, to indicate the type of target and the most effective ordnance. The field commander or a computer-aided expert system weighs factors such as which resources [helicopter, fighter plane, and artillery] are closest to target and which have the most suitable ammunition. This is *near-complete communication*.

Field tests of the digital battlefield have produced astounding results. Time-to-impact for artillery [the 'cycle-time'] has fallen from 50 minutes in map-by-radio co-ordination to nine minutes using digital business technologies. Potentially, the use of digital co-ordination technologies can reduce slack in systems by removing information-lag and reducing to the necessary physical time to perform a task. In other words, 'just-in-time' becomes almost 'zero-time'.

There are significant improvements in the decision cycle of observe – orient – decide – act. The technology alone is necessary, but not sufficient. To gain from it, it is essential that changes take place in cultures and behaviour so that the front-line – the soldier – becomes the starting point for operational decision-making. The army recognises that ultimately, only the field soldier knows the on-the-ground situation. While the army acts according to its missions and strategies, high *interactive capabilities* are essential to capture, communicate and act on every gram of information and intelligence. General Sullivan comments:

> 'Today it is difficult to forecast with any degree of certainty the theatre in which the Army may be deployed, the political or alliance conditions under which it will fight, the sequence of operations that it will follow, or where its mission will fall on the operational continuum. It is difficult to know the tactics, equipment, operational style, and overall modus operandi of one's enemy. One can neither script nor rehearse our battle plans.'

You cannot plan for the unforeseeable but you can act when it happens.

'What Desert Storm really taught us was that technology made it possible to shift the locus of decision-making from the field commander to the soldier. Intelligent and well-trained soldiers are thus the major source for sustainable battlefield advantage. They must direct battlefield operations. Cycle times need to be reduced immensely in order that operational results are immediately fed into the tactics and strategy of battle.

'In war you plan as best as you can. But what is predictable is that something always goes wrong...we should develop the ability to capitalise on these 'broken plays' and make this a source of sustainable competitive advantage.'

Decision-making is organised around the intelligence acquired by the front-line personnel.

4.2.2 *People and organising capabilities*

People and organising capability are focal points. General Sullivan is convinced that the Army's core competence resides in its organisational capabilities and for the next century will be built on quality people. He says:

'We must change the way we change...We have made all the initial steps to bring the power of the information age to logistics and war fighting. As we are building for the 21st century, quality people are the most important sources of sustainable competitive advantage.'

The general instigated a major transformation on six fronts: people; training; leadership; modernisation [technology]; doctrine, and force mix [i.e. combining the various army units as one cohesive force]. The transformation of *people* lies at the heart of the transformation of the US Army. A bureaucracy of *command and control* no longer surrounds the soldier. The shift in the locus of decision-making demands the highest skills from every soldier and his or her managers.

The ineffectiveness and costs of inadequate training are clear. In the case of fighter pilots, figures showed that 40% of all pilots were killed in their first three enemy engagements. A pilot who survived the first three would have a 90% probability of completing their combat tour. Training used to concentrate on 'transfer of knowledge' and 'conformity to standards'. Until recent years training had changed little since the beginning of the century. It used to be based on huge physical training centres that acted as teaching factories for mass-produced soldiers. The nearest the soldier got to understand the battlefield was a firing range.

Building the essential skills has meant a complete revision of the Army's recruitment and training methods. The core task was to emulate the real-world situation of combat. A *Combat Training Centre* placed officers and soldiers in mock combat sessions where every action was observed and recorded. Their uncompromising instructors had been the-best-in-their-class and could transfer hard-nosed, practical experience. In the real battlefield too often officers take decisions without really understanding the results of their actions in modern warfare. Digital recordings of the full battlefield, and observer-controllers, revealed the failing of officers in painful *After-Action Reviews*. A unit's chain of command was exposed to having its failure explained, step-by-step, to subordinates. For the officers the experience was gruelling and very humbling, but very successful in increasing a unit's ability to survive and win in combat.

4.2.3 Lessons for Total Action

This case of the US military is a model of Total Action. It is a large organisation which, until recent times, had been trapped in Fatal Inaction. When the army emerged from the Vietnam war it was on the edge of 'institutional bankruptcy'. Through the 1970s it had to fight to maintain its existence, with undisciplinable personnel fighting physically between themselves. In 1980, the failed attempt to rescue American hostages held in Iran made the organisational confusion especially visible: a large, over-centralised organisation with poor communication ability and the inability to plan effectively. People's eyes were opened. The organisation had to attract world-class soldiers and develop first-class military equipment. This meant breaking down the internal competition between those pushing their own pet products.

The 1973 Arab-Israeli war was a further, very strong stimulus for rapid change. The military saw the revolution in precision as advanced technologies narrowed the 'circular error probability' of bombing and allowed accurate long-range gunnery. Military leaders recognised that they must develop these advanced technologies, but *the technology alone would not be enough*. The Soviets, then the enemy, had a greater arsenal of weapons of equal or better quality. The best warfare technology was seen as essential but the *doctrine* had to change: *leadership* must be as important as firepower, the fighting qualities of soldiers had to be improved so that they acted to their full capacity with a superior war-fighting method.

Question: How did the military tackle the 4Ps?

Question: Digital battlefield technologies helped the US military understand that they must re-engineer their forces around three core processes: the soldier, organisational capability and logistics. How does this fit the Total Action model?

4.3   The American Airlines case

When American Airlines [sometimes "AA"] installed its first SABRE terminal in a travel agency in May 1976 few observers could have foreseen the dramatic impact that this would have on the airline business[3]. What began, back in 1959, as an internal 'factory' to process airline reservations, was to evolve into today's travel value cluster, used by travel professionals, corporations, and consumers all over the world. In addition to airline tickets, people now use it to make car and hotel reservations; to order theatre tickets, bon voyage gifts, flowers

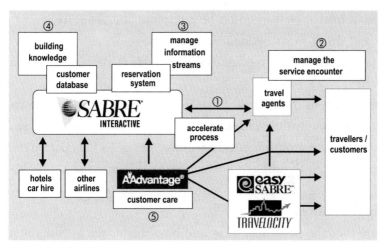

Fig. 4.1. The five steps

and other travel-related goods and services. The system grew, as figure
4.1 shows, through five main steps:

- accelerate the processes;
- manage the service encounter;
- capture information streams;
- build knowledge of the customer;
- build the value cluster – be an industry infomediary.

4.3.1   Accelerate the process
A passenger airline can be regarded as having two critical webs of activity:

- *operational management*
    when the aircraft sits at the gate preparing for an imminent take
    off, the web of information streams and physical processes essential
    to its departure coincide in space and time. In additional to all the
    information relating to flight logistics:
    - all passengers must be on board;
    - their luggage must be in the hold;
    - it must attributed to the individual passengers;

- the passenger inventory must be complete and accurate;
- food and drink must be loaded;
- special dietary needs requested by individual passengers must be satisfied.

Any breakdown in the chains of information and activity can cause significant delays, resulting in the loss of a take-off slot and increased cost to the airline, not to mention inconvenience to the customers. Many of us know the misery of unaccounted luggage in the hold.

– *winning the customers*

to ensure that the passenger buys and buys again, the airline must perform immaculately for that passenger. This means ensuring that the operational failures do not harm the passenger's loyalty and that data on the passenger can be used to tailor behaviour, as far as possible, toward his or her requirements.

There is, of course, a clear link between operational and customer-focused information. Clear information on customers and their preferences and behaviour is essential for planning the operational processes and determining how they must change to further improve performance with the customer.

SABRE – the Semi-Automated Business Research Environment – was conceived in the 1950's to *speed up the process* of reservations. In the early days it took 12 different people performing more than a dozen separate steps over a three-hour period – longer than the flight itself – to complete a booking for a round-trip reservation from New York to Buffalo. American Airlines saw the opportunity to use information technology to speed up this process and make it more effective. From a travel agent's terminal, SABRE was able to complete a seat reservation and make the associated data available to any location on the system. However, this capability – the automation of the reservation factory – although advanced for its time was only the initial step in the SABRE saga.

4.3.2 Manage the service encounter

In the 1970s passengers were not really the airline's main 'customers'. Thousands of travel agents managed the business of booking flight reservations and, as a result, had an important influence on which airlines passengers would use. If the passenger wished to fly from New York to San Francisco, the agent had to consult the individual timetables of airlines flying between the two cities [a practice which remains largely in force today]. Then, having chosen a specific flight by a specific airline, the agent had to contact the airline [telephone or telex], determine seat availability, and make the reservation with the reservation personnel of the airline. The ticket could then be issued and mailed to the agent or the customer. Should there be no seats available, the process would begin again.

By putting the on-line reservations terminal on the travel agent's desk, American Airlines made it easier to buy from AA than any of its competitors. It had gained a competitive advantage. The travel agent was able to find out immediately whether seats were available on a specific flight, confirm the reservation and issue a ticket. SABRE was able to bring the customer instant gratification and save the agent a significant amount of time.

4.3.3 Capture information streams

While American Airlines was managing information streams for its own passengers, the company opened up SABRE to allow its competitors' reservations to be made. This was an important step in establishing reservations, and information technology, as new business streams for American Airlines. By 1986, the company made twice as much profit from SABRE as it did from flying passengers.

In essence, the company was becoming an 'electronic market' – linking numerous buyers [agents and individuals] and suppliers [airlines] through SABRE to complete their transactions. Today, SABRE provides the schedule information for more than 700 airlines and has reservation and ticketing capability for 400+. From this position, American Airlines are in a position to capture vital data on most airline passengers: who flies, from where, to where, when, how often and at what putative price. They made the key step of deriving customer information from the automated reservation factory.

4.3.4   Build knowledge of the customer

All customers are important but some are more important than others. 70% of full-fare travel revenues came from less than 500,000 passengers. American's Airlines' intent was to capture the vital data on these passengers and use it to ensure that they became real customers...they bought more than once. The AAdvantage programme, launched in 1981, was the precursor of today's loyalty programmes. AAdvantage sought to win the hearts [and valuable business] of repeat passengers by giving them preferential treatment. These customers became the centre of American Airlines' attention for marketing and service and for product development – the company's new source of performance improvement and innovation.

With the existing SABRE infrastructure in place, the airline was in a position to capture data on these passengers. American Airlines persuaded regular flyers to 'join the club' by giving additional information beyond that available through SABRE and by offering the reward of free flights. American Airlines was thus able to develop the flying history and profile of each target passenger, giving the opportunity to differentiate service. American Airlines had redefined customer service in the airline industry. Or, to be precise, they had changed the premium customers' expectation of customer service. Through tangibles like their frequent flyer programme, seating allocations, and executive lounges [and things less tangible like knowing your name and preferences], AA forced competitive airlines, at least to match their services.

Without American Airlines' information and telecommunications infrastructure and the years of corporate learning, the competitors were at a disadvantage. They had to emulate the automated system by using manual systems, employing data-entry personnel to enter customer information. They had enormous difficulties in matching customer data to their reservation systems, making numerous errors and, of course, suffering from greatly increased costs in the attempt to match American Airlines' capabilities.

American Airlines outsmarted its competitors. Regarded initially as a short-term attack on market share, SABRE was dismissed by many at first as a white elephant. The competitors had failed to realise American Airlines' real goal of gathering passenger date and re-using it to win continuing business. Their customer care programme created data which could be fed directly into improving the performance of its operational webs of activity.

In addition, by gathering data to rationalise its routing and schedules, American Airlines was able to become the leader in 'hubbing', working from a base outside the expensive New York area. American Airlines did much more than simply automate the factory. It squeezed information out of the factory processes and the customer access points and translated it into corporate knowledge.

Delta Airlines: taking care of customers by name

The problems which Delta Airlines faced in the mid to late 1990s have been well reported. The airline had to undertake a major transformation of its total organisation – inwards from the customer – and put in place information platforms that could cut through the organisational chimneys. However, visitors to the Operations Centre in Atlanta cannot fail to be impressed. They find a calm centre of activities relating to the scheduling and in-flight monitoring of all Delta's aircraft, and the environment – weather etc – through which they fly. The centre is an operational informational and activity hub for the whole airline, resulting in lines and clusters of people and highly interactive and user-oriented information displayed on video walls and computer screens.

When you click on the dot representing a specific aircraft, its previous route, its routing and its 'contents' can be displayed, down to the names of the Delta personnel and each passenger on board. This is essential operational data. It is also of extremely high value in serving the passengers. There is storm around Atlanta, which is not unusual. As a result many flights are delayed and, indeed, many have to be re-routed. At this point, the Operations Centre can take charge of managing the requirements of each passenger on the flight. Automatically, the system looks up individual passenger priorities [class, frequent flyer, etc] and any connecting flights. It then allocates them to alternative flights on Delta [or competitors'] aircraft. If the flight is re-routed, each passenger's return to Atlanta will be organised in the same tailored way. This can be communicated directly to the aircraft in-flight and each passenger will be informed.

Question: How do the SABRE and the Delta cases illustrate the role of access to information?

Question: How would you describe American Airlines' compelling vision?

4.3.5   Build the value cluster – become the industry infomediary

In 1985, American Airlines introduced easySABRE to allow personal computer users access to the SABRE system. At the same time, its reservation capabilities were expanded to include railways, tour companies, passenger ferries, and cruise line as well as hotels [31,800 today] and car rental [50 companies]. Today, easySABRE is accessible on the Internet and, through its alliance with Travelocity[4], has expanded from being a flight reservation system to become an infomediary for travel by integrating reservation functions within an overall travel planning system. It creates the travel-related value cluster illustrated in figure 4.2.

From the single point of the computer screen, almost anywhere in the world, the easySABRE or Travelocity subscriber is able to check information on possible flights, prices, and seat availability. Travellers can make reservations on over 400 airlines. FlightfinderSM will seek out the three lowest cost itineraries for a chosen destination and allow the potential flyer to make the necessary hotel and car rental reservations. Travelocity provides information such as climate, currency, facilities,

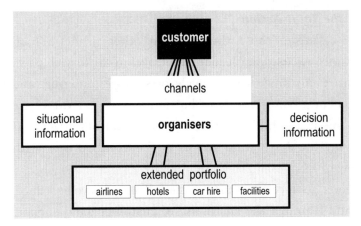

Fig. 4.2. The travel value cluster

entertainment, restaurants, and points of interest on cities and holiday locations.

American Airlines is acting on an extended portfolio. Rather than maintaining a basic portfolio of 'flying the passenger, comfortably, from A to B', American is catering for the customer's wider travel requirements by providing additional services: hotels, car hire, and other facilities. Acting as an infomediary, American Airlines is providing information such as pricing and availability to help the customer decide, supported by the situational information that helps the decision process.

From the Travelocity web page, or other infomediaries offering 'travel' as part of their information portfolio, it is easy to transfer to easySABRE. Interest can then be transformed into transaction – seduction becomes order. And, while this takes place, the three components of interaction are brought into play:

- communication between the potential vendor and traveller;
- information exchange between the parties; and
- goals of the two parties – find holiday, deliver holiday – are more easily achieved.

4.3.6   Lessons for Total Action

It is not easy to call American Airlines [or any other airline] a Total Action organisation. A customer leader [the travel agent or web page] manages the entire customer service cycle of seeking, ordering, and receiving a ticket for a confirmed seat, but few passengers would see real customer focus in the full customer service cycle from arriving at check-in to leaving the destination airport at the expected time with one's own luggage.

The SABRE actions lie in certain parts of the full service cycle: seduce, order and pay and [through the smart use of customer data] support and renew. The critical part – fulfil – is a major challenge, particularly as such fulfilment involves numerous other parties such as the airport facilities, customs and immigration, and air traffic control for which no individual airline can guarantee service levels. However, it is the airline's responsibility [and challenge] to act on relevant information from these parties to keep passengers informed [delays, new times of departure, etc]. This seems to be major sources of failure in many so-called, advanced airports. The clear lesson is that *access to customer information can drive the organisation.*

Question: How does American Airlines manage the customer access channels?

Question: How could American Airlines put to use more of the Total Action model?

Question: If you were a competing airline, what would you do?

4.4   Banking on information: the First Direct case

The financial industry is an information industry. Financial services are derivatives of the financial organisations' ability to manage money or, more importantly, manage information about money. At the heart of this industry are the retail banks: those organisations with a seeming monopoly over the exchange of payments between individuals and organisations. Banks lie at the heart of one of the key information streams between organisations and between people: that of payments and information about payments.

4.4.1 The 'misery' of banking

For many years the banks have been able to take for granted what their 'product' was, and what their customers expected of them. They were amongst the first to implement digital business technologies – and began to discover how important it is to implement the technologies wholeheartedly.

Who pays whom?

In 1992, the authors were working with a national inter-bank payment-clearing house. This *payment factory*, established and owned by the banking community, managed the transfer of funds from one bank to another. To facilitate this payment management, they worked to well-agreed message standards. The payment-clearing house (let us call them *PayClear*) had a simple question: 'what can Payment EDI mean for us and for our banking community?'

They had seen the gradual adoption of 'product' and 'logistics' EDI and the beginnings of payment EDI messages being adopted and provided by some of the EDI Value Adding Network providers (for example GE Information Services and IBM Information Network) and some banks (for example, Chase Manhattan). They could see a strategic threat or opportunity for themselves and for their owners, the banks.

This, apparently straightforward, question (what can payment EDI mean for us?) reveals the difficulties in integrating relevant transaction data when more than two parties are involved. The payment chain, payer-bank-*PayClear*-bank-payee, appears, at first sight, straightforward but it is characterised by the following difficulties which are inherent in automating the majority of chains.

All the banking portion of the chain 'sees' is the payment together with the necessary data on the payer and payee. Both the payer and the recipient, in particular, require more data to be transferred across the chain. The

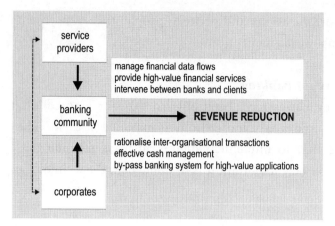

Fig. 4.3. Disintermediation of the banks

payer and the payment recipient want to ensure that vital data is preserved across the payment transfer between them and their banks. This vital data is the remittance information.

Remittance information is very important for the recipient. It can be plugged into the financial application engines to reconcile payment receipts with invoices and credit notes. It is fairly straightforward for the payer to package this information into the payment message (or send it alongside) and hand it over, electronically to the bank. However, here the difficulties begin.

To preserve this vital data across the chain, Customer A packages up the message and transfers it to Bank A, who then transfers it through PayClear to Bank B who sends it to Customer B. There are, of course, alternatives.

When Customer A initiates the payment, an electronic remittance message could be sent directly to Customer B: "the cheque's on the network, this is what it is for!" But this means that the payment and the information about the payment are separated, and will arrive at different times and thus increase the co-ordination/reconciliation overhead for Customer B thus defeating the object of the exercise.

Why, then, does the payment chain route not work:

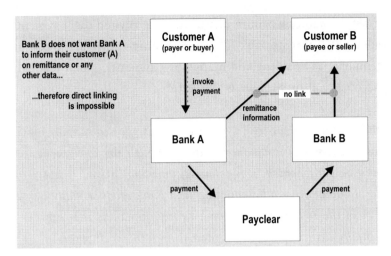

Fig. 4.4. The information impasse

- Bank A receives the electronic payment instruction and the associated remittance data.
- Bank A wants to send the remittance data directly to Customer B while triggering the payment chain through PayClear.

This means:

- again, the payment and the remittance data are separated, and
- Bank A wants to establish a transaction relationship with Customer B.

This is unacceptable to Bank B which regards this as the entry point for stealing the customer. Therefore:

- Bank B suggests that Bank A sends the remittance data to it, so that it can send the data on to Customer B.

This is unacceptable to Bank A since it would begin an informational relationship between Bank B and Customer A.

This form of 'Catch 22'[5], although simplified, began to defeat the initiative. For both banks, using *PayClear* as the remittance-data manager was unacceptable since they both believed that this would increase the clearing house's position. The clearing house would be making the first steps in becoming a 'managed transaction integrator' not only for financial transactions but also ultimately for the majority of transactions.

In this example the banking community cannot see beyond the 'payment' and its associated 'information'. They are seeing their 'business' at that time primarily as enabling and managing payments, albeit through PayClear. As observed by Steiner & Teixeira[6]:

> '65% of the (banking) industry's system expenses goes to support of just this one function of funds movement. Although the movement of funds can be complicated, it is relatively mechanical and is not the source of competitive differentiation in a bank product. Only around 10% of the industry's expense goes into functions that are even potentially distinctive. Their systems' investment supports services which are commodities.'

The authors' experience supports this statement. In one large, international bank some 90% of IT investment was in back office functions, with less than 5% invested in customer-facing systems. This lack of focus on the 'customer' seems to be reflected in consumers' perceptions of the quality of their retail bankers. For many corporate and individual customers today, banks are the organisations they love to hate. They need them... but they know that the banks could perform better. Today, few consumers would view the banks as centres of excellence for building customer leadership and moving into Total Action. We have seen a dramatic shift in the banks' relationship with their customers in recent years, particularly as, driven by deregulation, competition for financial services has intensified and brought many 'near banks' to market. Today you find supermarket chains and other organisations, particularly those with strong and positive customer branding', moving into banking territory.

The financial superstore

Marks and Spencer, the UK retailer, has spent some £600 million [$1,080 million] on information technology over the past ten years. The value of such data was recognised in 1984 when it introduced its 'account card' and did not allow other credit cards to be used in its stores. The card gave the customer a perception of the benefits of loyalty and became very popular. By gathering data on customer spending patterns, Marks and Spencer were able to develop into a major UK financial services provider: personal loans, investment, life assurance, and pensions. They have 5 million account card holders and, since 1984, have advanced £2.5 billion [$4.5 billion] in personal loans and manage investments of over £400 million [$720 million]. This brought an operating profit of £37.5 million [$67.5 million] in 1997.

Such a retailer has at least two major advantages over the retail bank:

- The bank sees its customer's payments and receipts while the retailer sees the customer's financial behaviour. It has more complete information on the customer than the bank;
- while many banks are physically withdrawing from the customer – closing down their High Street real estate and replacing it with ATMs [Automated Teller Machines], telephone banking, and, seemingly remote, financial call centres.

In parallel, there is the advent of 'Internet banking' and 'Internet payments' [digital cash] which, although little used today has the possibility of revolutionising the ways in which people handle their 'cash' and make payments. It is, perhaps, a generalisation to say that the main retail banks have been slow to respond to the possibilities of digital business technologies being consumed in re-engineering their museums of payment factories. At least one bank, First Direct in the UK took a lead in redefining the simplicity of telephone banking to move towards making the customer its locus of decision making.

This is your telephone bank, we're here to help you

Telephone banking, like home shopping, has been a discussion rather than an action point for many years. The possibilities were first discussed at the end of the 1980s when the power of telecommunication alongside computing was becoming highly visible. Then, it would appear, few people wanted to bank by phone. The technology platforms, despite videotex and the 'tone' telephone, were not really in place. They demanded the fingers of a safecracker and the numeric memory of intelligent log tables to achieve access.

Telephone banking emerged as an adjunct to standard banking: 'You can telephone us', during office hours, perform some digital gymnastics with your telephone keypad or subject yourself to the discipline of our voice 'recognition' system [which would never work after a good grape-inspired dinner].

However, First Direct's telephone banking has been successful. A new bank, albeit a subsidiary of Midland Bank, in 1998 they had over 850,000 customers increasing at a rate of 12,500 each month. In addition, First Direct has become the UK's most recommended bank. 90% of its customers have stated that they are 'extremely' or 'very satisfied' with 86% saying that banking with them was better than banking with other banks. 81% of their customers recommended them to their friends[7].

4.4.2 *Making it work for the customer*

First Direct clearly identified its target market and the value which user-friendly telephone banking might offer for customers in this market. The target market was those individuals, 'DINKIES' [Double Income – No Kids] who had income to be managed and very little time to deal with the restrictions of traditional banking practices. Market research showed the company some important characteristics of these customers [and many others, it turned out]:

- They did not like queuing: busy, working individuals could only visit their bank when their contemporaries could visit the bank. The result: queues.
- Banks were closed when they wanted to use them: out of office hours, including the weekends.

- They did not like 'telephone banking': the telephone-keypad gymnastics and voice-activated computer systems were not to their liking. They could not 'interact' effectively. Most times, they wanted to talk with an intelligent person, not a dumb computer.
- They did not believe that banks offered value for money: the UK retail banking industry was dominated by the main four banks: Barclays, Lloyds, Midland and National Westminster with little, if any difference, between them. The Dinkies regarded them all as bureaucratic, arrogant, distant, and unresponsive.

For First Direct, the 'value' they wanted to offer their customer was ease of access, at any time, from any place – by telephone. Mike Siddons, Director of Operations, said:

'We had to be able to respond in seconds, not minutes... normal banking procedures simply did not apply. We had to create a workable system that would be the servant, not the master, of those who would be using it. It had to be a high performance system that was both flexible and easy to use... within a single phone call.'[8]

First Direct has one main access channel: the telephone [although, in 1998, it is being augmented by PC access]. Paper communication is still necessary, and the customer needs to use ATMs to draw cash. But, for the rest, it is that single telephone call. To achieve this First Direct had to define and manage the linkages between the company's 'banking representatives' and the back-office. As figure 4.5 shows, the banking representative had to be able to manage the full interaction with the customer, drawing on real-time back office or specialist support where necessary. So digital business technologies had to provide all necessary support to the banking representative's customer screen. From this screen the representative managed the total interaction. To achieve this, the banking representative needs:

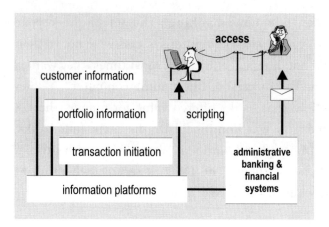

Fig. 4.5. Manage the interaction — and deliver the back office financial factory

- *customer information* — which authenticates the caller and provides information about the caller's history and position, so the banking representative can react to requests;
- *portfolio information* — which matches the services the bank provides to the specific requests of the caller; and
- *transaction initiation* — which can initiate financial transactions, send [paper] communication to the customer, and monitor subsequent progress.

These are supported by:

- *scripting* — navigation information delivered to the banking representative to guide their responses to the customer's questions or requests and steer the customer in the appropriate direction;
- *information platforms* — electronic linkages to the necessary information sources and transaction machines; and
- *linkages* — to the back office – the administrative, banking and financial systems. For example, linking to the payment factories to enact payments and to the administrative system to evoke postal delivery of information to the customer.

4.4.3   *Information empowers customer leadership*

These are the elements of customer leadership – being the director of events with the customer and with the organisation itself. First Direct's banking representative is the *customer leader* for this specific customer throughout this interaction. She or he has the information support to react to and pro-act with the customer's decision-making process. The banking representative is able to direct and work with the specific customer action team for this specific transaction. When the customer contacts the bank again, he or she may deal with a different banking representative who has the same [updated] information on the customer and the same capabilities. This is one-stop managing.

For the duration of the customer's interaction, the individual who answers the telephone becomes the customer leader. He or she can complete the transaction and invoke fulfilment under clearly-defined boundaries, acting according to a menu-driven 'script'. Where the customer leader needs to move beyond the mandate, specialist, or management, support can be brought on-line in real time.

This customer leader is not permanently associated with the specific customer. He or she becomes the customer leader as soon as the phone rings. The process of *customer leadership has been captured in the information platforms,* in software, databases and applications. The platforms then deliver it to the customer dashboard. The banking representative becomes a temporary co-ordinator of the demand chain, relinquishing this position when the call is finished, or abdicating it when a specialist takes over. Customer leadership is preserved in the software.

In First Direct, customer leadership depends entirely on the information platforms. Without them, the person answering the telephone is powerless. As figure 4.6 shows, the customer leader depends entirely on access to information.

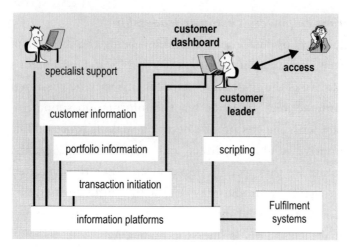

Fig. 4.6. First Direct's customer leader

4.4.4 Lessons for Total Action

First Direct made a total commitment to defining business according to new customer-driven performance parameters. In this case, the traditional access channels to and from the customer, the retail branches, were not augmented with an additional channel – the telephone. Rather, First Direct based its entire business on the premise that the customer would be their locus of decision-making. All business operations would be driven from that one point of contact. To achieve this, the parent company [Midland Bank] established a new and separate business that drew very little from existing resources: other than a set of computer tapes which contained disparate information on customers ('accounts') and which the IT department had always been unable to use sensibly for marketing or customer care purposes! The bank recognised that existing staff and organising capabilities would be ill matched to the new operations. A new and separate organisation – such as First Direct – avoided the 'outside-in' collision but meant that they would in fact cannibalise their own customer base and marketplace.

First Direct is, in reality, a sophisticated call centre, supported by excellent organisational capabilities. Few organisations will take the leap of faith that Midland Bank made in establishing First Direct and betting its business on the ability to excel in customer leadership on a single access channel. First Direct gives the indicators for what customer leadership can be but, it fact, it did not solve any of Midland Bank's problems in interfacing with its customers, until they could draw on the learning from First Direct and embed it back into the parent organisation.

Question: What kind of risk was Midland undertaking when it launched First Direct?

Question: Were the banking representatives just 'telephone operators'? What would it take to give a normal telephone operator this kind of responsibility?

Question: How could the 'back office' maintain its identity and role?

4.5   Total Action policing

You would expect your police force to be a Total Action organisation. All activities of the police have to be linked directly to our need for a secure place to work and live. In practice this does not appear to be the case. Enforcing the law is the goal that determines the ways police works and thinks. Traditionally a very hierarchical and task-oriented organisation, police forces give their officers little, if any, incentive to see you as a 'customer'.

Digital business technologies, however, are beginning to have a major impact on police work. These can give an officer instant access to information and almost complete communications. A fundamental rethink of the essence of policing becomes both possible and necessary as police forces face the risk of failure in meeting the requirements of a modern society.

The following examples come from a number of police organisations in Europe, whose strategic leaders are trying to forge new approaches to satisfy the increasing demands that the public places on them. We are particularly grateful to the Police Department of Rotterdam, The Netherlands, for allowing us to share some of their learning. As one of the largest regional police forces in Europe, they take responsibility for security and policing of a very densely populated area which includes the largest port in the world. However, this is a composite case, and the views we express depend on a more general assessment of how police forces should use the concepts of Total Action.

It is easy to see that a police force must be an organisation with fluid, self-organising capabilities. It must always be able to organise rapidly and effectively to deal with an incident. It must have complete communication on the specific incident and the ability rapidly and accurately to build profiles of individuals and organisations. Indeed, one can see extremely advanced incident-centred communication and information capabilities. Yet, behind these, in day-to-day operational activities, the intelligent linking of necessary information and the organisation of resources – creating the 'business network' – can be considerably less effective.

4.5.1   Find out who is the 'customer'?

To achieve Total Action one mandate is that the customer becomes the locus of decision-making. The first requirement, therefore, is to ask the question *who is our customer*? One police chief responded: *"We don't have customers: we have security risks, criminals, and victims."*

What view – if any – does your local police officer have on you as an individual? Does he or she actually know you? Are you seen as a prospect, a customer? Or are you seen as a potential criminal, security risk, a witness, or victim? How do you interact with the police? Are they able to bring together all the information that they have on you when they need it? Police can collect a wide range of information about you from their various 'points of contact' – a fine for speeding, your report of a car theft. Do they use this information so that they have a complete view on your situation and can act with immaculate precision when you need them?

In modern society, 'security' has become a well-recognised need. The clever use of information can help provide a safe and secure environment for working and living. To achieve this security, the police will have to handle information in new ways.

Value to you – the 'customer'

Imagine you have come home from the cinema after 10 pm to find your door smashed, papers strewn about, windows broken, and valuables missing. You immediately call the police. They arrive about 10:30 pm, take down some details and give you the name of a locksmith. The locksmith shows up at midnight and fixes the broken locks, but he can't do much about the broken windows or door. The next day you go to your local police station to make your statement, not only to help catch the burglars but also because you need a police report for insurance cover. There is a queue and you wait. Eventually, one of the duty officers is ready to see you. No, they are not aware of the burglary. They cannot make a report since, in fact, your house is located in a different district. Yes, it is true that this police station is the nearest to your home, but it is in a different district.

When you insist, your details are taken and sent to the appropriate unit. This will take time and, still you do not have the necessary police report for insurance. At this point you wish your insurance company would simply take your word! Finally you decide to go to the other police station and, after waiting and explaining the situation again, you get a copy of the report. Back home you start calling the insurance company, the glazier and the carpenter to repair the windows and door. You also tell your neighbours that there are burglars in the area.

During this upheaval, you would never expect that the police would see you as a 'customer'. The night after the burglary, when you looked out of your window, you would have been pleased and reassured by the sight of a police car keeping its eye on your neighbourhood, but you see none. Why do you now feel so uneasy when, previously, you have always felt secure in your home? If it is so easy to break into your house, you should perhaps take the advice of the locksmith and get a professional security company to put in an alarm system. In hindsight you feel that the police, in fact, did very little: not around when you needed them, not very helpful, no surveillance today, and what felt like bureaucratic harassment at the station. What do the police do that is of real 'value' to you?

What does this tell us about your interaction with the police?

- *reactive rather than pro-active behaviour* — The police can only react to the call. When they arrive they have only limited information and find it difficult to follow-up with necessary support.
- *no instant sharing of information* — Information is not instantly communicated throughout the police organisation. It is reported into the 'appropriate channel'. This channel, unfortunately, is responsible for an area different to that of the police station which is physically closest to you. So the police officer in that station is unaware of what has happened despite the necessary information being captured somewhere else.
- *a poor service encounter* — When you report the burglary the encounter is typically bureaucratic. No attempt is made to help you, to build your feeling of security nor to give you information on prevention.
- *alternative service providers* — New relevant information services can develop: based on the Neighbourhood Watch linking to the locksmith, glazier, etc., and the insurance company. The police are not involved in this and are not managing their interaction to prevent burglaries or to help in the cycle of events following a burglary.

The example shows how the behaviour of the police can breed a dissatisfied public. It is a simple example but, as more violence and insecurity develops, members of the public will start organising their own security and adopt ways which are not purely digital but also offer physical security.

A customer in the digital world

Consider the possibilities in a digital world. You are now aware of the local Neighbourhood Watch. In fact, that evening, there is an e-mail waiting for you asking you to check their web site. You check in and introduce yourself by name and address. Your house is a red dot [with many others] on a digital map of the area. You click on it and there are details on the burglary. It shows that you are not yet 'registered' with the local Neighbourhood Watch but links you to advice on prevention, security companies, locksmiths, glaziers, carpenters, and all kinds of potential suppliers in the area.

You click on the other dots. Some list the goods that have been stolen, the ones which have been found, together with the status of the police inquiry. Somehow this makes you uneasy. Any criminal could check this page, it's a useful source of knowledge for them. It could be their site! Why are the police so absent on the net? If they were using it effectively, police officers would be able to collect all kinds of information on your case and relate this to other events in your area. They could keep you informed constantly on what they were doing to catch the thieves. They could give advice on how to avoid this happening again. Next time you have a security issue, will you first call the police, or the neighbourhood-watch web site?

The police solve, at best, around 5% of all criminal offences with 40% of reported criminal offences brought to trial, with an approximate 50% success rate. A senior police officer commented on the statistics to a group of colleagues:

> 'Our task must be to regain our position – to inspire confidence that we will look after the public... otherwise law abiding citizens will take justice into their own hands. We have a monopoly on law enforcement, but with such figures we would be bankrupt in a normal business sense. This monopoly will do us no good. It distorts our efforts, our mindset. We concentrate on intervention

and repression. We act after the event has taken place and we play
hardly any role in prevention and risk assessment. We need a new
mindset, a new frame of thinking on security and risk, on what it
means to provide our modern community a secure place to work,
live and relax.'[9]

Many interactions with the police come about as a result of distressing
individual experiences: a car crash, a speeding ticket, a burglary. Most
people will agree that we need the police, but few today relate this
need to a positive personal experience. Members of the police need a
new understanding of the individual's requirements from policing [what
they deliver]. The need for security is fundamental. If the police force
is to be more than an instrument of law enforcement, it must try to
manage a *value chain of security risks* that increase the individual's
feelings of security. With such a mindset, the police force helps its
'customers' to:

- assess risks;
- assist in risk reduction;
- be warned early on developing risks;
- prevent crime and assist the justice system.

For the police to move 'closer to the customer' in this value chain,
they need more information about their own front-line activities. They
must shift the locus of decision-making to their customer – the individual
in society:

- develop a *customer-centred mindset* to gain a collective understanding
  of what people expect from a 'secure place of work and living' and
  the role which the police must play in achieving this; and
- improve *interactive capabilities* to handle and manage a variety of
  information in very unpredictable situations.

All activity must be directed to the 'customer' of this value chain. In most policing this is not the case. The police do not regard the individual as a 'customer'. The individual does not pay or have choice. The argument that 'the government is our boss and our customer' distorts the whole system.

4.5.2 All activity is not customer activity

A police force can suffer the debilities of a commercial organisation. Applying the 'timesheet test' revealed that a disproportionate amount of police officers' time was being lost on internal administrative matters, and a great deal of the remaining time was, quite simply, being wasted. The public wants to see the police officer on the street; he or she wants to be 'in the office'. A senior police officer noted that the officer gains higher reward and recognition by being in the office.

> 'We have 12 salary scales to reward our people. Three of these are
> for officers on the street. These are in no way the highest scales. For
> financial reward, everyone wants to make their careers in headquar-
> ters. They do not want to be out on the street.'

Most of the waste results from 'idling time'. The police force is a reactive organisation and it is difficult to predict when they will be needed. As a result, personnel are scheduled for attendance in case they are needed rather than called on when required. With limited budgets and, as a result, limited personnel, such a timetable determines the police force's quality of service! Thus the organisation works on 'best-efforts' and measures itself on the frantic activities of its workforce – 'you had better look busy' – rather than on their outcomes.

4.5.3 The wrong metrics...it's not what you do!

Like many commercial organisations, the police are task-oriented and budget-driven. Their performance indicators come straight from Taylor-type thinking: do this task and spend no more than X amount of time and Y amount of money doing it. Attempts to create accountability by results rarely succeed. For example, if given the target: "The police must increase the percentage of reported crime solved by x%", the normal response would simply be to make it difficult to report a crime!

Budget cultures tend to obscure and distort what is really important to the organisation. In one case the police units had their time budgeted according to differing activities: a percentage a time to be spent on crime matters, another percentage on environmental issues, traffic management, and so on. Unfortunately, these percentages were averaged for the whole force and bore no relationship to the specific areas which individual units were serving. Thus a unit which could prove it had no environmental problems still had to allocate a fixed percentage of its available resource to handle non-existent problems. The result: lengthy discussions about the error of the norm and the unreliability of the data...and the suggestion that someone, somewhere, must be mad and put in prison.

4.5.4   Connect information systems

When the police force is operational, reacting to an event, they draw on and apply advanced communication and information systems. In such situations, rapid and effective communication underpins success. As in the modern army, the police officer at the front line has to become a locus of decision making; the operational units can then be connected together in an information network to ensure that every leverage in resources can be obtained.

The police arriving at our burgled house probably received all the necessary data from the emergency services [a call centre], displayed on a screen in the police car. Is this good information, though? They receive only the address and description of the reported incident. By weaving together a number of information systems, the police could send additional information valuable to the officer and to the victim. For example, information on the house, its location, who lives there, the owner, possible alarm systems and details on house contents. This data would influence how the police might enter the house as well as what support and after-care the victim might receive.

Given effective information systems centring on the police activity at the incident, the police officer could take statements on the spot, file them electronically, and establish links to other databases which give more information on the crime history in the area. At the same time, an electronic report might be communicated to the insurance company and relevant data forwarded to the neighbourhood watch site on the Internet. The police systems could also alert a locksmith, and send an information package on burglary prevention. Just this extra attentiveness, visible surveillance the next day or a comforting telephone call from a police officer would improve the willingness of the local community 'to help the police to do its duty'...to assist the police to manage the value chain.

In many police departments the non-operational – the back office – information and telecommunication systems do not support any integrated workflow. While platforms are in place, they are disparate, as they often are in the commercial world. They were created for disjoint functions, each having a different 'owner'. As police forces recognise that the customer must be the locus of decision making, the need increases for rethinking and integrating these information platforms.

4.5.5 Make the customer the locus of decision making

A chief of police together with his senior staff formulated their vision on the future of policing:

> 'The central theme must be the sense of security of our citizens. We must define this more clearly, and develop a method to measure it. But the essence is: we want our citizens to rate our performance and the score must be at least rated good or very good.'

To achieve this they decided to form community teams [their customer action teams]. These teams were to be fully accountable for the quantitative performance scores that were determined by the citizens. Each community team comprised five officers, and one named community police officer served as the customer leader. Each team served some 1,200 citizens, based on a population of 1.2 million people and a police resource of 5,000.

The community teams serve in a similar way to a general practitioner, a dentist, or a sales representative in a specific sales area. They rely on specialist support from the organisation, but the community police officer is in charge. Thus the locus of decision making moves towards the individual citizen. Simple as this may seem, it was a completely new way of working for this police force. Important features of the new approach are *individual accountability; ownership of the value chain* and *streamlined work methods and style.*

Individual accountability for results

Police community team members are measured on the results of their individual actions. They have to know their 'customer group' on a one-to-one basis and achieve a satisfactory score on objective and subjective criteria such as the public's perceptions and beliefs. At the same time, the community teams must manage within the 'rules of the game': the agreed standards of behaviour and performance. The budget is one of these standards.

> '*You must not see this budget as something we, the central authorities, give to you. Take our total budget, divide it by the number of people we serve, then you can see what an average family pays for police services. Your task is to give them the belief that they get the best possible value for that money. You must also think of new, resourceful ways to increase the value that you can give the public.*'

This means that the community teams must make sure they raise realistic expectations with their 'customers' and that they can meet these within agreed parameters.

Directing the value chain

The prime consideration in police activities must be their 'societal relevance'. The importance of law enforcement in creating a safe and secure environment needs re-assessment. Repressive actions, in proportion to the efforts needed to carry them out, do not increase people's sense of security. Preventative and pro-active actions are more important.

> 'In the complex security market, we, the police must sharply define our position and role. Our key point of attention is the solution and prevention of security risks. We should not have an inventory of work that creates bottlenecks in other parts of the chain. If we know there are no cells available, we should resolve this first, or change the repression methods that we use. If our police work results in criminal proceedings by the Justice Department, we must avoid duplications and time delays. In partnership with the Justice Department and the courts, we can greatly reduce the lead times in penal proceedings.'

Such a policy gives the police direction of the security value chain, engaging other parties as partners in the network. Based on good interaction with the public, the police force can greatly enhance its effectiveness:

> 'Do not think of us as 5,000 police agents trying to catch 30,000 criminals. Think of us as professionals who solicit the public's help to create a safe and secure environment. So it is us with the help of 1.2 million citizens...!'

As figure 4.7 shows, new roles emerge. The management of the security value chain encourages new relationships with strategic partners such as the fire department, hospitals, etc, as well as many more parties who play a vital role in creating or preventing security risks.

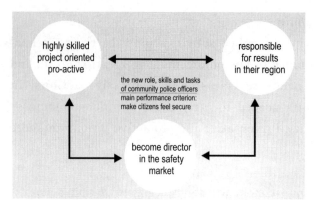

Fig. 4.7. Winning with the citizen

Changing the style and work methods of the individual agent

You may not always like what they do, but they do it professionally. To improve the service encounter with the police, officers must know more and work differently. They must know more because there will be an increased range of activities to be undertaken.

'Every time you encounter the police you must be impressed by its professionalism and citizen-orientation.'

If you are robbed 'your' police agent should know almost instantly and be able to help you. A personal relationship, based on mutual respect and growing trust, should develop between the officer and the people whom he or she serves. At the same time, the individual agent must be able to call on the strengths of the whole police department. This puts entirely new requirements on the speed of information handling. Near complete communications are required. At any moment, the individual agent and the back-up organisation must know what is happening and what must be done.

Improving the service encounter requires a different way of working. Pro-active and multi-skilled police agents need to 'project manage' all the activities essential to their community groups. On the one hand, the community team, close to the citizens being served, is always accessible and is known to them. On the other hand, the team must engage necessary specialists for short-term, ad hoc project assignments. This is very different from being part of a specialised compartment of the police organisation, dedicated to specific kinds of incident. As the community team takes care of the customer, it must interface on the customer's behalf with the various 'counters' of the police bureaucracy, and organise them for the sake of the customer. The team will have to develop the collective strength of the organisation on an ad hoc project basis to act on specific situations. The team will try to break down the walls between the various functional units – crime, drugs, murder, traffic offences – but it has little hierarchical authority.

Such project-based integration of the various units, under the direction of the community officer, parallels the integration of the 'chimneys' in the modern army, or the functional chimneys that challenge companies as they implement account management and customer leadership. The situations are the same despite the apparent radical differences between the organisations.

4.5.6   Create the information platforms

The customer cannot become the locus of decision if the individual police officer does not have access to the appropriate community information. Like American Airlines, the agent needs to capture all information relevant to that community and from it derive new understanding to provide premium services. In order to do this, access to information must be organised so that it is accessible from different functional angles. This necessity has proved to be a major stumbling block. The barriers to achieving this include:

- *incompatibility* — Vital information needed by the basic police processes, personnel, and finances were in a variety of incompatible computer systems. In one case, we found over 250 application systems. Some had the same purpose or application but they were using different data dictionaries. They could not be made to inter-operate.

– *inadequate telecommunications* — The different telecommunication networks could not be interconnected. On voice networks there was no number portability. For each location, as well as for different mobile networks, there were different numbers. They needed one number for each individual irrespective of the network.

– *limited access to necessary information* — The agent on the move was unable to access vital information. It existed on a limited number of physical terminals. In one case, a visual recognition system for suspects, officers had to go physically to the computer system since the network didn't have the bandwidth for transfer to other devices. In other cases, new networks had been built, dedicated to a single application. To add further applications meant serious increases in costs.

– *inadequate security* — The enormous diversity in networks and applications resulted in weaknesses in data and system security. As attempts were made to integrate applications and make them mobile, ensuring security was found to be nearly impossible.

– *skills shortfalls or the lack of technical personnel* — The current IT people lacked the skills to develop the integrated 'enterprise information system'. Nor did they understand how they must, as information professionals, contribute to the actions necessary at the customer front.

These archipelagos of disjointed information systems, resulting in disparate operations, need to be transformed into a common, shared information environment. This requires:

– a cohesive communications network;
– clear definition and realisation of information platforms;

- information tools which support the police officer, independent of location; and
- a service organisation which guarantees predetermined levels of information and communications service against agreed costs.

Without a basic 'enterprise highway' you can't interlink incompatible information systems. Internet-based technologies allow data to be shared between distributed systems. Creation of such a highway may seem straightforward but most organisations still have not managed to organise the 'electronic socket in the wall' to provide 'bandwidth on demand' [data dial tone]. Hence information on demand, managed by a remote control centre, seems a long way away.

Even today, most police IT effort concentrates on organising the basic, existing, information platforms and defining and developing automated processes for the core activities of their organisation. They are cleaning up the mess. The managed capture and use of community data on security risks is an exception. Usually data on criminals is captured. It is essential, but has very little value for the police as a service organisation.

Empowering the community officer with modern digital tools will prove essential for future police work. Through such empowerment, the police officer in our example could arrive at the scene of the burglary with full knowledge of the situation and location: the person who called, the house, the possible routes of the burglars and the possible receivers. The neighbourhood watch and the locksmith could be informed. The victim would not need to report to the police station since the insurance company could be informed automatically. The victim could receive a completed electronic claim form. Next day, the victim could also receive preventive advice from the police. The local community could meanwhile be asked to watch for certain people and call or e-mail a special number, should anything need to be reported.

4.5.7 *Lessons for Total Action*

Behind these examples are influential individuals in major police forces who recognise that their organisations *must* change. In reality, this recognition was driven by the belief that:

- the police organisations were not performing effectively; and
- they must fully understand the new digital business technologies, and the impact they could have on police performance.

These drivers have not been discussed. Rather, the discussion centres on *the discovery of the customer* and *what performance for this customer will mean*. This is true 'discovery'. Until police forces perceive their role in the value chain of security risks, there is no customer. Identifying the individual in society and the requirements which this individual, as a 'customer', would place on policing, helps identify and define a customer service cycle. With a clearly defined mission for the customer, the police are able to create customer leaders and customer action teams, with clear customer-centred performance metrics. By examining the requirements of these teams, the information support and the platforms to deliver this support can then be determined.

This shift to the customer as the locus of decision-making does not centre on the customer at the police incident. Rather it develops a mindset of ongoing customer-attentiveness and learning. Having established this, a police force can improve its handling of events that demand police attention. To achieve this, the police have to enact a major programme of *engaging outside-in* in order that every officer – from the lowest to the highest could understand, commit to, and act on Total Action policing.

Question: How is the police mindset formed – and how can it be focused more on the customer?

Question: If you were a senior police officer with budget and performance targets, how would you spend your IT money?

Question: How does the public communicate its performance expectations to the police?

4.6   Trying to connect to you

Imagine an organisation with the total power of telecommunications in its embrace – almost for free – and holding the telephone numbers of every individual and company in the country. It is cash rich and has had its market protected by the government. Yet it is still trying to understand the difference between a subscriber and a customer!

This is the situation of many large national PTOs: the Public Telecommunications Operators. Despite these advantages, they have enormous difficulties identifying and recognising the individual customer and bringing together all the customer data that they hold in their various information systems. They also have enormous problems in their commercial handling of the individual customer and their service differentiation on a one-to-one basis. As a result most PTO's gamble on large-scale, mass produced services. Could they do it more smartly and more effectively in the digital age?

Since the mid-1980's the PTOs have been in a maelstrom of change. In most countries they had been comfortable government departments with a total monopoly of the provision of telephone services and equipment. They had a simple mission: give everyone a telephone – in every home and every business! You could have any colour telephone you wanted, as long as it was black. The PTOs did not have customers; they had 'subscribers'. As an individual or company you subscribed to the telephone service and were identified not by your name but by the numbers of your telephone lines.

Most PTOs were fatally inactive, autistic organisations. It was not necessary to be otherwise. The customer had no choice. PTOs had no competition except in the area of data communication [of which they seemed to have little understanding].

POW!

When the forces of deregulation and liberalisation hit the PTOs in the 1980s, most were unprepared for the incredible impact that new intense competition, new customer expectations, and the dramatic explosion in telecommunications would have. They faced three major problems:

- *recognising the individual customer* — They had not built any systematic understanding of their customers. In the past they simply did not have to do so. Moreover, when they turned their attention to the customer, the information that they held was fragmented and not aligned to the information that they really needed.
- *customising services* — They had little experience providing and managing differentiated services to individual customers. Their systems were not geared to support such differentiation. Worse yet, they could not build the co-operation between sales, product management and the network factory.
- *persistent autistic behaviour* — Despite many stressful efforts they continued to find it difficult to organise and direct their behaviour into a structured and meaningful dialogue with the customer.

In addition to deregulation and liberalisation of the marketplace, some PTOs were also faced with privatisation. Their owners – the governments – took them to the stock exchange. Their inadequacies [above] meant they were not performing to – or capable of measuring – the targets which a business required. In many, there were no concepts of margins, profitability and accountability, according to basic business understanding.

The challenges were manifold and even today they are troublesome, despite dramatic improvements in the performances of many of these organisations. For this case, we will concentrate on the most important advantages Total Action can bring to such an organisation: *discovering the customer, redefining the portfolio* and *engaging outside-in.*

4.6.1   *Recognise the individual customer*

Sir Iain Vallance, chairman of BT, stated in the mid 1980s:

'I want my customers to buy from us, not because they have to, but because they want to!'

BT [then 'British Telecom'] was one of the first to feel the sting of real competition. In rapid succession in the early 1980s it was:

– split off from the Post Office [now 'Royal Mail'];
– 'liberalised', to end the government monopoly and encourage competition; and
– privatised.

BT embarked on this new competitive route with the knowledge that, whatever it did, it must lose market share. The key questions were: *Which market share?* and *How much larger would the new market be?* BT lost customers. At first it lost business with the large organisations. Subsequently, it lost business with individual consumers. The loss of customers certainly helped to energise its organisation. When the customer needs the supplier more than the supplier needs the customer, the supplier's life is sweet. When the situation is reversed, the normal market dependency in which the supplier needs the customer, life gets tougher for the complacent supplier.

Any organisation that is not subjected to the verdict of a dissatisfied customer develops a strong inward view of the customer, as an interrupt to their business process. This logic is not easy to change. For decades the PTOs' main concerns had been technical: to build nation-wide networks and to link these at the borders, while providing the population at large with telephones.

The key questions are: *Who are my customers?* and *How must I perform with these customers?*

To confront such an organisation with the reality of its customers is a painful challenge. Once the customers can 'vote with their feet', a PTO must really perform. If it fails, it cannot go back to the old monopoly, but the customers can go on to the new competitors. The organisation, its monopoly withdrawn, needs a clear and deep understanding of the requirements of each customer. It must also make every customer important. The company must be ready to make itself really dependent on the customer's rating of its performance.

Many PTOs began prioritising their customers by determining their value in terms of revenue. Though it may seem strange, they often had difficulty calculating the actual financial value of their largest customers, since their financial systems recorded the wrong data in the wrong place. They could measure turnover per telephone line, but they could not link the revenue data for customers with different sites and, hence, different invoicing addresses. Thus large customers were just a list of subscriber numbers held in different regional centres, with no way of combining the data.

As financial data became more available, the operator's view began to shift regarding which private person or company was really important. The telephone bill of the 'little old lady in Tennessee selling tennis shoes' seems unimportant for the big operator. But when you see she is receiving regular high-value telephone calls from her family in New Zealand her importance becomes more evident. A PTO always deals with at least two customers, the caller and the called, and must understand how to derive value out of the connection between the two [even if one is not its own customer]. This understanding has stimulated a great deal of research into the calling behaviour of customers, resulting in new services like call waiting, redirect, voice mail, and operator assistance, which connect calls that previously would have failed. New revenue has grown. Attention to and knowledge of the individual customer has become vital.

You're only as good as your last encounter!

The CEO of a large international company once visited a PTO shop to buy a cordless telephone for his use at home. The shop staff managed the sales encounter with insensitivity. The next day, when the company's procurement committee was considering competing bids for a large international telecommunications project, the CEO's opinion on the quality of service of the PTO was sufficient to ensure that it lost the bid.

Prioritising, or segmenting, the customer base is not a straightforward task. The largest organisations became the focus of attention for the PTOs. These organisations bring very high revenues and are the first victims of attack by competitors hoping to cream off the easiest and most profitable business. Such 'key accounts' demand high levels of qualified attentiveness from their telecommunications providers. They want to discuss business solutions rather than telecommunications products. PTOs, in order to ring-fence these accounts from competition, were forced to introduce key account management practices. However, the structured analysis of these individual key accounts has seldom resulted in systematic understanding of customers.

True account management requires more than the skills of a super sales person. Account managers are seldom the customer leaders who, on the basis of a deep understanding of the business of the customer and the operator, act as the directors of the business with company-wide support and respect. In practice, they seldom had a mandate in the organisation and found it difficult to link to the PTO back offices that were still working according to the rules and behaviour of the days of the monopoly.

Concentrating on the top customer segment is fraught by risks. It is difficult to get an accurate assessment of profitability because of the PTO's archaic cost accounting systems. After all, in the past, such systems had not been necessary. It is certainly evident that such customers' profitability to the PTO is under pressure from competition, despite the dramatic increase in the market.

Successful operators are now paying keen attention to the full spectrum of customers, from the largest to the smallest, by trying to apply customer management methods to all segments. However, so long as the top management refers to the communications channels with the customer base as market 'outlets', then PTOs will find it difficult to succeed.

4.6.2 Organise customer information

With so little customer-orientation, it is not surprising that customer information is fragmented across many different systems, each optimised for its own function. There is one system for network planning, one for network service management, another for subscribing to the service, one for repair, and yet further systems for invoicing and debt collection. Such systems multiply as each service demands it's own: telephones, data network, leased lines, mobile phones, etc. In some PTOs customer data has been tucked away in almost 300 different computer systems that are near impossible to link together.

Operators were forced to invest enormous amounts of money to bring customer data together in customer care and billing systems. [BT alone spent over £1.5 billion [$2.7 billion] and many years of effort and training to implement one of Europe's largest computer system to combine billing, repair, and sales systems.] The goal is to collect and link all customer data, preferably in one huge data warehouse, to simplify basic customer processes [service, subscription, billing, collection, complaint handling]. Such a system can also help create new services based on 'caring' for the customer. Hooked to the intelligent network control centres of the infrastructure, a unified system supports services such as BT's 'Friends and Family' [call five telephone numbers at a discount] as well as loyalty programmes. The idea is sound. If you can combine the data on customers and data on your operations, you can derive many new and customised services. These services can generate high value to the customer at low cost to you, particularly when you stimulate off-peak traffic and increase call and call completion rates.

PTO's have taken some time to recognise the value of squeezing customer data out of their operational systems. Every time somebody lifts the telephone handset details are being recorded in the computer exchange on the location of the caller [i.e. the line – not the person], the called party, call path and duration. These Call Detail Records – CDR's -have the same comparable value as the flight records do for an airline. If you know who calls from where to whom, when and where, and for how long, then you have a formidable source of information and advantage. However, because of the enormous volume and inaccessibly of this data, operators ignored it for many years. Then, when it became important, they found it extremely costly even to decide what they must do with it. And, of course, today the regulator does not allow unfair use of this data.

While the PTOs grappled with the technical challenges, the account managers, who were educated, trained, and engaged in a fight for the customer's business, found that customer data, now essential for them, was inaccessible.

To solve this, some PTOs adopted the customer dashboard approach, providing the electronic workbench for account planning and management and are positioned to extract data from, and provide data to, the various computer systems of the network factory and product houses.

4.6.3   Customise services

PTO systems are not typically geared to support differentiated services to the individual customer. Even more important, the co-operation and linkages between sales, product management and the network factory are usually inadequate.

If your business is to provide each of your customers a link to another [telecommunications, post, transport, banking], each time they are linked you have opportunities to derive revenue from both parties. An example is call redirect or forwarding. Without call redirect the call results in only a single revenue. With call redirect, the operator receives revenue from the initial call [the caller pays] and then revenue for the link between the called destination and the redirected destination [the called party pays]. One failed call becomes two connected calls. The network operator charges twice and has two satisfied customers.

To customise service on an individual basis, it would be helpful to know the individual customer's identity and the reasons for the call. If the customer uses a calling card, then the PTO has more chance to know the identity of the caller. However, the identity of the called party is not known. Even the giant systems for customer service can't register the individual caller or called party in the way that American Airlines can recognise the individual passenger.

4.6.4   Connect sales to the factory

While the necessary systems are gradually being moved into place, a number of PTOs have suffered shorter-term problems in providing customised services. Too often they suffer poor organisational interfaces between sales or customer service and the product management and marketing departments. The problem deepens as one looks to the interfaces with the network department ['the factory']. The difficulties tend to stem from the organisational history and from individual and departmental inexperience of new roles. This poor sales-to-factory interface leads to:

- *misunderstandings of the portfolio* of services from a customer viewpoint, resulting in gaps and duplications, nonsensical pricing schemes, poorly set priorities and increasing operational problems in the handling of today's services and the introduction of new ones.
- *divergence in processes* as the various individual product or service managers try to use traditional product and innovation management practices, which are not geared to today's telecommunications business.
- *waste of internal energy* as product managers try to take over sales

and marketing responsibilities to create 'shelf space' for their own products. Since a customer 'solution' may not include their products, they prefer to manage and control their own channels. This results in customer confusion and, for the sales front, lack of clarity on portfolio strategies.

Interface issues can be addressed in part by establishing strong portfolio management and marketing functions. The marketing department can act as the intelligent two-way interface between the marketplace and the portfolio – between the sales front and the product houses – rather than concerning themselves with 'marketing communications'. Product managers and innovation managers need new kinds of connection and support, as figure 4.8 illustrates. As an intelligent interface, marketing brings various parties together to manage customer and portfolio priorities and set the important directions. It can then, at a minimum:

– position individual products within an overall portfolio;
– construct packages for individual customer groups;
– monitor the product planning and release processes.

4.6.5   Overcome autistic behaviour

In one PTO, a few executives had begun to recognise the need for action, to survive the onslaught of competition. Three significant action lines were necessary:

– ensure that executives – the board and top management – fully understood the immediate and longer term impact of their lack of performance;
– put account management in place for those largest customers who would be attacked by competition; then
– use the account management as an operational blueprint, by translating the concepts of customer leaders and customer action teams in real high-performance activities.

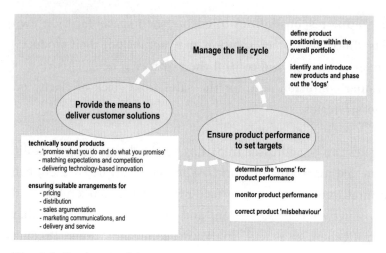

Fig. 4.8. Product and innovation management

To ensure that they built up a programme concentrating on sustainable performance improvement [rather than a set of 'sheep dip' account management training courses], the top executives had to be seen to lead the changes. This point was found to be very important. Initial steps to introduce 'account management' had been, in essence, to send some chosen people to account management courses and then expect them to perform. This was doomed to failure, since these new account managers returned to the organisation to discover that:

– they were not recognised by the remainder of the organisation;
– there were no support processes for them;
– while they had acquired the mechanical skills of account management, they were unable to translate these, developing the understanding of the [largest] customers, to determine 'telecommunications solutions'.

This kind of tokenism happens too frequently. It simply demonstrates to those trying to implement change the limited strategic understanding of how to embed new behaviour into the organisation – to engage it outside-in.

Open the eyes

One top executive recognised the symptoms of failure in their current approach. He was convinced that his colleagues needed a significant shock to open their eyes to the reality of their situation and, as a result, define and agree to the steps that must be taken. A brief but extremely sharp presentation to the board highlighted, with supporting evidence:

- the dramatic changes taking place in the telecommunications world and the resulting expectations of their customers;
- the views of a selected number of important customers on the PTO's performance;
- the internal behaviour of the organisation;
- the routes to improvement which they should adopt.

Most board members accepted the dramatic changes that were taking place but found difficulty in accepting that they would have any impact in the near future. They felt secure with the customers and felt they would have time to re-organise to deal with the threat of competition. However, their eyes were truly opened when presented with the extremely strong views of a major customer, views that they had to believe.

The PTOs performance had been analysed through the eyes of one of the country's largest customers, a steel company [selected because, unlike financial institutions, its dependency on telecommunication would not be so obvious]. The customer's overall outlook was captured through a series of video interviews with different people: the operational telecommunications manager, the IT director, a top manager, and ordinary users. The PTO board members were shocked. They learned that in the eyes of one of their biggest and best customers:

- *we have no secure relationship* — the core telecommunication services were essential to the functioning of the steel business. However, according to a senior steel manager, they had no meaningful relationship with the PTO. Performance on present services was seen, at best, as adequate, and at worst, as unprofessional. The PTO had been the 'best of no choice'. But with the advent of competition, the steel company had begun discussions on potential alternatives for certain services. At first, the PTO board members thought the customer 'only complained about high prices, non-delivery, and so forth'. When the steel executive went on to present serious defaults on a number of key contractual agreements, the eyes of board members started to open. Until then, they had been totally unaware of this situation. It had been lost, or hidden, in the internal mechanics of their organisation.

– *we have no strong position with this customer* — while the board had felt that they had a strong position with most major customers, they saw that their position had no real significance. A look at the customer's total current and planned spend on telecommunications made it clear that they were not winning all that they could, and that there were ample opportunities for new revenue. They were losing out on data networking and systems, where the customer spend was significantly larger than in the traditional telephone budgets and was growing much faster. In addition, they could see that their contact surface was made up of only those who had direct responsibility for 'telephones'. They had no links to the business motivators and decision-makers – a very serious defect.

The internal behaviour of their own organisation opened the PTO board members' eyes even wider. Despite frequent communications between account management, product management and network departments, the best efforts of the isolated account manager had found no way of improving the PTO's position significantly. They were exhibiting inconsistent behaviour to the steel customer, and presented no managed interface, or co-ordinated approach. The relationship was event driven, with unplanned and independent responses. The internal organisation was either unaware of the steel company or denied that they had any responsibility for the customer. Nobody knew the true overall turnover or portfolio position.

The operational service managers were taking their own decisions. When the service manager for telephones decided to introduce itemised billing, every subscriber got an itemised bill. As a result, the steel company received a large number of post bags containing thousands of telephone bills – one for each telephone line!

The board launched further investigation with other customers, plus internal activity and performance audits, so managers throughout the PTO could clearly see:

- misunderstanding of the mission and business of the customer;
- inability to give meaning to the mission of the PTO at the customer level;
- no acceptance of the nature of account management nor of the mandate for a customer team;
- customer perceptions of the PTO way out of line with its high ambitions and self-image;
- lack of customer understanding of the portfolio;
- inadequate skill to handle the new competitive environment, both in front line people and back office support;
- no information support of any operational or strategic significance for front line people;
- very little financial information on the PTO's business with the customer;
- naiveté on the role, threats, and attacks of competition.

The key messages were very clear:

- the PTO's current performance with its customers was inadequate: they were not giving value for money [the performance gap];
- significant opportunities for new revenue were not being exploited

[the opportunity gap] and so they would lose out to competition in the new markets.

Begin customer action

Not only had this to be understood but it had to be acted upon. Many key action lines were required, with special attention to account management, information handling, performance measurement, and the link between product management and the sales front. Rather than embark on a multitude of projects to bring the 'big fix', the PTO adopted the approach of engaging outside-in.

Other programmes were assessing the organisational structure and the governance of the organisation but, to move quickly, they decided to implement a form of customer action teams – centring on the account manager. The account managers were to develop as customer leaders while their account teams acted as customer action teams. These customer action teams differed in some ways from the concept introduced earlier in this book. Rather than being formed to ensure fulfilment, their mandate was to determine how the organisation must act in managing the customer service cycle.

Their goals were to

- gain a deep understanding of the customer's businesses;
- determine the requirements for telecommunications solutions;
- assess the performance of the PTO's portfolio with respect to these requirements;
- determine the back-office support required to succeed with the customer, as well as sales support [a new organisation which was being formed], ways to eliminate autism in the product house, and develop connections with the 'factory' – the providers of the network and its services;

- 'open the eyes to the customer' by bringing the reality of the customer step-by-step closer to each member of the organisation.

This approach had two great benefits:

- the account management organisation became a learning organisation. By working outside-in they were able to identify how they must organise and be supported to deliver to the customer;
- the account management organisation became visible and was able to act on top management mandates. It gained respect from [most of] the organisation as capabilities developed and performance improved.

This was no six-month project. After five years this process of revitalisation and performance-driven change continues. The PTO has faced continuing changes in its marketplace and customer base. As it 'took control' of the top accounts and, indeed, protected most of them from competition, it found that smaller national customers were being attacked. And, as new operators were licensed and mobile telephony took off, the whole customer surface had to be addressed, with consistent, managed processes – and then, in response to these inputs, essential changes in organisational behaviour had to be put into place.

When the sales front and the sales back-office had been improved, the process and information links between sales and the product houses showed up as a significant barrier to competing effectively. Then, suddenly, the customers were talking about the Internet and Intranets. Very low-cost international telephony started to emerge. The rules of market behaviour of only two years before had been destroyed.

The importance of management development

It is not only the staff who find it difficult to change their behaviour. Moving management attitudes is often more difficult. One PTO executive commented:

> 'Why should we expect that managers whose careers have been
> created by the system would be prepared to destroy that very
> system?'

It takes more than courage to inflict a crisis on yourself. Yet many companies are forced into crisis by competitors taking valuable market share, shareholders selling, or bankers calling in the loans. The decline begins with dissatisfied customers who, given the opportunity, take their revenge. Competition gives them the opportunity.

Telecommunications operators have traditionally tended to reward mechanistic and efficiency-oriented managers, rather than those who are customer-oriented. In fact, the financial systems that link capital effectiveness to performance with the customers are often lacking. The result is a 'fair' management culture that bases employees' success and careers on their effort, rather than on what they achieve according to clear performance criteria. In today's competitive environment, in a PTO or any other kind of organisation, it is vital that top management creates a culture that puts the customer first, one that has sound indicators of financial performance.

Understanding the theory is necessary but it is not sufficient. On completing their 'change management' workshops, managers understand what must be done and are committed. But when they return to their day-to-day misery of internally driven activities, the enthusiasm dissipates like an ice cube in a cup of hot coffee:

> 'Yes, I understand the theory of change and performance
> improvement, but I cannot do it...alone.'

When the PTO managers left their eye-opener workshop, each carried his or her action plans. These had the goal of developing the ability to create and sustain action in their real life situations. As they moved to engage their personnel they developed 'action skills' and learned to communicate effectively.

These managers were learning how to handle and communicate self-inflicted crisis. They also knew that their employees had to learn to handle the crisis. Strong 'change agents' were needed who could drive the necessary change into the organisation. This was the role of the customer action teams. The action team managers took on the pivotal role. They were willing and able to realise change, from varying levels in the organisation – not all close to the top. Top management took on the task of identifying, supporting and developing them. Their qualifications included:

- the persistent belief that revitalisation would be the key to competitiveness;
- the ability to articulate this conviction in the form of a credible and compelling vision; and
- the skill to implement this vision through a consistent pattern of words and behaviour.

Management has a critical role in directing and guiding people as they are engaged outside-in. Ultimately, the managers must answer three questions: what is *my* value to the customer, what is *my* value to my organisation and what is *my* value to my people.

4.6.6 Lessons for Total Action

The essence of this PTO case [built from a number of different experiences] is that a well-constructed approach of *engaging outside-in* is fundamental to achieving true organisational transformation. It is not a process of re-organising which can result in:

- internal debates and discussions which burn and waste internal energy;
- a shift in the balance of power – new managers – but no new behaviour and performance;
- confusion as continual waves of re-organisation and re-structuring

sweep through the organisation. These can kill initiative ['we can't do anything until after the next re-organisation'] and confusion ['If my manager phones, get his name' or 'I don't know what we will be doing next week'];
- lack of confidence in management – a lot of noise and nothing happens – there is no leadership.

Outside-in engagement centres on the customer. Performance with the customer, in turn, results in:

- clarity – we know what we must achieve – with the urge for external focus;
- immediate emotional pain – usually frustration at what is not being done – which is replaced by a concentration of energy on the customer;
- initiative – continuing solution seeking, whose results can eventually be embedded in formula and process;
- attention to key competencies and, often more importantly, the key incompetencies – what must we do and what can we do to succeed with the customer;
- trust in leadership – management leads the clearly defined learning process and its implementation.

In the PTO, customer leaders and customer action teams began to move the locus of decision-making towards the customer. The full shift had to come over time as the PTO organised for true customer action teams – the 'virtual' account teams with responsibility for managing and directing the customer service cycle. This has not yet been achieved but as the true requirements of the customer front are identified and the support and delivery mechanisms are being put in place – particularly the information handling tools driven by the account manager's customer dashboard – the PTO is getting closer to Total Action.

4.7   The postman never rings twice

Traditionally, few see the postal service as a commercial, customer-centred enterprise with a high potential for growth. Set against the high-tech image projected by courier companies and logistics services, the post office may look like a survivor of the old 'physical' world that is being displaced by fax, e-mail, and other forms of electronic communications.

Such a view is misleading. Forward-thinking postal organisations are, in fact, transforming themselves into new businesses, building their core activities and rediscovering their customers. Some are applying the concepts of Total Action with innovative zeal. They have begun to establish advanced customer management practices and to attune their systems to trace and record every customer activity. They have done these things because, in future, the postman must do more than ring the recipient's doorbell. He or she must actively call on a customer.

This case is based, in particular, on the authors' experiences with TNT Post Group in The Netherlands. Experience with other postal organisations supports our contention that a number of post organisations are responding effectively to new market forces, so to some extent this, like the preceding PTOs, is also a composite case.

The Post has a very clear and simple customer: the person who addresses the letter, places a stamp on it and puts it into the mailbox. Post also has some more complicated customers: those who send large amounts of mail and, in some cases, subcontract parts of their business to the postal organisation. Like their sister organisations, the PTOs, national postal organisations grew up protected by monopoly and have developed advanced technologies in their 'factories' for collecting, sorting, and delivering envelopes and parcels.

Today's postal service is an organisation with a known, but many times anonymous customer. To cope with competitive forces, Post needs to:

– ensure that its internal agenda is driven by the customer – the locus
of decision-making; and

– develop interactive capabilities to support complete communication
and instant information access, providing value to the customer
and to Post.

4.7.1   Who is my customer?

Post has traditionally taken the view: 'Our customer is important, but
we can only serve this customer well if the factory runs effectively!'
Protected by the monopoly, the postal organisations were able to
concentrate managerial attention on the core business: time-based,
low-cost mass collection, sorting and distribution of envelopes and parcels.
They scrutinised every step of the mail process and created a low-
cost, effective, and standardised service. The only forms of customisation were the discounts to large users and the differentiation between
first and second class stamps.

A significant portion of Post business is created, and paid for, by a
relatively small number of large companies. For example, in the
Netherlands some 50 organisations account for about 40% of the PTT
Post turnover. These customers get special treatment in the way of
discounts, but only as long as the standards of the core service are not
compromised! There is also a strong belief that the demand for postal
service is determined by factors which Post cannot influence:

> 'If a bank decides to reduce significantly the numbers of statements
> which it mails to its customers, there is nothing we, Post, can do.
> We have lost the business!'

Characteristically, production-oriented companies invest little in
customer skills, and they certainly do not invest systematically. Postal
organisations often lack the systematic knowledge about their customers
to be able to understand and act upon developments in the customer's

business which could be important to Post. When the bank reduces the number of statements it mails to customers, Post might offer the bank the use of a call centre [managed by Post] with direct print-and-mail facilities so bank customers could receive their statements within 24 hours.

The standard account management approach should be to turn such a problem into a customer solution. However, this is frequently not the case. Smart account managers, identifying such an opportunity, may face difficulties: their organisation often does not understand them. In the view of the organisation accounts managers are there to sell, not to think!

For any organisation, the first phase of 'discovering the customer' is setting up customer teams and customer leaders with a wide and strong mandate to serve the customer across the different organisational chimneys. This step can conflict with the formation of business units [letter mail, printed mail, parcel, courier, international, etc] that tends to accompany 'commercial thinking'. As each business unit claims responsibility for the customer, potential synergy is lost. More important, each business unit has to build its own understanding of the customer, and may have little incentive to share this insight with the remainder of the company. While all are dependent on the same factory, differing interpretations of the same customer can become a more serious problem than confusion alone. If the real motivations and requirements of the customer become invisible then the organisation cannot innovate.

Develop common understanding of the customer

This concerns the interactive capabilities of the company. How well is the postal organisation able to share information on the customer and to communicate and act on specific customer events? For Post, apart from the invoicing systems, the customers are mostly invisible. There is a sender who pays, using a stamp or a franking machine, and there is the recipient. The production system requires only the recipient's postal address to determine the route through the system. But the data on the customer is not captured. They do not know who sends, or receives, which post, when and where. However, is this knowledge really important?

If you look at Post's business to see the patterns of communications among its customers, then you are looking at it in an unaccustomed manner. When such a view is taken, it creates a new demand for information. Post is commercially obliged to find out why customers communicate. In principle, Post has significant data on its customer's – physical –communications patterns. It has long overlooked the importance and value of this information, but now, if it can gain this understanding it can create new business and new revenues.

Post needs to examine the traffic flows and study the reasons for customer communications. Once these are known, the communications patterns of customers can be optimised, to the advantage of the customers and to that of Post. The senders and the recipients can be turned into sources of revenue. As the large customers increasingly view 'mail' as an integral part of their communications systems, such opportunities arise.

If Post knows why organisations send mail and how it is received then it can strengthen its relationships with the customer, with potential to integrate postal processes and customer processes. For example, when the recipient does not open the mail or internal organisational procedures delay its delivery to the end recipient, Post's ability to 'deliver anywhere within 24 hours' is wasted. To create value and effectiveness for customers, Post needs such knowledge of customer behaviour.

The significant potential for improved postal processes will only be tapped through better understanding of the customer, and customisation of the post factory to meet specific customer requirements.

Understand the customer's business

Suppose you ran a large mail order company. Would you regard Post as an important business partner? Post distributes your catalogues,

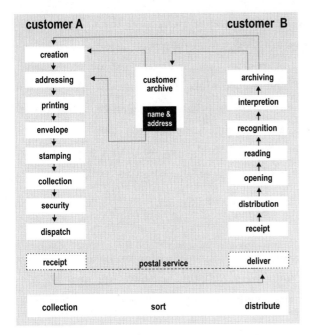

Fig. 4.9. Post as a logistical service provider

brings letters and cheques from your customers, and delivers your
invoices. It may, or may not, deliver parcels for you.

Post's proposal

In spring the customer leader from Post organises a meeting with you
and makes a proposal along these lines: 'couldn't we distribute an extra
feature catalogue about holidays for you this year? Summer is coming
and it's not usually the best season in your line of business. We believe
that we can create extra business for you. We will help you with all the
necessary paper handling and make sure the catalogues get to the right
people at the right time. We can handle warehousing and we can guarantee
overnight delivery from receiving the order. Our drivers could take payments
from your customers. Also we can process every letter your customers
send you by scanning and sending it on, electronically, to your correct
administrative centre. Our call centre could handle any overflow from
yours. If you run regional radio or television advertising campaigns, we

can deliver the catalogues at the best time to support the campaigns. Of course, you could also use our direct mail database.'

The customer leader has a short, but clear, business case, which promises a hit rate of 2%. For you, this would make good business sense in view of the proposed bundled price. Post's fulfilment capabilities for orders on your new Internet site are also suggested.

'But', you ask yourself, 'can Post really deliver what they propose?' You want to qualify Post's capabilities by asking the Post customer leader more questions:

- Apart from the suggested seasonal factor, why are these extra catalogues such a good idea?
- Could you be more exact about the part Post is going to play in our fulfilment cycle? You know very well that we have our own logistics resources and this scheme would put you in competition with them?

If the customer leader wants you to accept this proposal, he or she must demonstrate a deep understanding of the mail order business, your own business. Without this knowledge the proposal could not have been made, the suggestion would have been meaningless. Without an understanding of the processes in your own enterprise, or the demonstration of knowledge and experience that can be applied directly, the customer leader is unlikely to persuade you to proceed with the proposal.

Acceptance of the Post would result in an increase of its budget the mail order company allocated to Post. Post proposes a unique combination of services from its portfolio. The alignment of the processes of the two companies is no simple undertaking, so it is not an offer which Post might find easy to fulfil. Dealing with the required volume of material may well prove straightforward, but timed overnight catalogue delivery? However the scanning, and the linkage of information and transactions will not be so easy for Post since it runs a 'standard factory' which cannot easily tackle individual customer demands without upheaval and costs.

Post will need to deploy all the organising capabilities it can find and embed a means for mobilising them within its organisation. The role of the customer leader is to match the capabilities and the capacities of Post to the needs of the customer.

This role requires:

- Understanding the customer's value proposition – what is the mail order company proposing to its customers and why is it valuable?
- Aligning the ambitions of the supplier with those of the customer – is the mail order company interested in a more complete fulfilment service and a specific action for the 'holiday theme'? If so can Post do it?
- Matching what is valuable to the customer with the capabilities of the organisation – starting from the point of the customer solution, can Post, in fact, deliver this? Does it lie in today's portfolio? Might it be constructed and developed to be a standard service, optimised for mail order and other organisations with similar needs?
- Action-orientation – the customer leader must have the drive of an entrepreneur and business leader, be a project leader with a goal-reaching mentality and show skills of leadership which operate in a non-hierarchical setting, in a systematic and planned way.

If Post's customer leader is to lead in a systematic and planned way, he or she needs this systematic understanding of the mail order business as well as deep knowledge of Post's capabilities. Under the principles of Total Action, every customer – large and small – merits a customer leader.

The information that the customer leader needed about the mail order company included:

- the number of packages to be ordered by mail, delivered and returned;
- the related communications flows (letters and telephone calls); and

– the number and destinations of the catalogues to be distributed.

In addition, the customer leader needed to understand three relationships:

– who would respond to the catalogue?
– how was the delivery process to be organised?
– how was the interaction to be completed?

Post might have put that information into the customer leader's hand, but the data had not been captured. It had not been viewed as important since it did not fit the logic of the business.

Post had tended not to view customer information as important. Basic information on individual customers was regularly dispersed over many information systems, and could not be unlocked easily. Yet access to such information was a core condition for successful Total Action. The kinds of information linkages necessary were:

– a product coding system containing the various services and their price codes;
– a customer contract system;
– an invoicing system;
– a contract management system;
– a payment system;
– a financial reporting system;
– a business counter system; and
– a management reporting system.

From these, Post was able to build the customer dashboard to develop their interactive capabilities from the newly-understood customer front.

4.7.2   Build a customer dashboard

Post recognised that a vital move would be gathering and managing information on their largest customers. Account management had been established but it needed to be reinforced in terms of information tools and linkages inside Post.

The customer dashboard approach was adopted with the first orientation on the account manager and team. [They called it 'the account navigator'.] This dashboard supported the account manager in systematic and detailed planning of strategic goals, tactical actions and revenue targets. In addition, it had to support the account manager in maintaining and monitoring account plans.

The dashboard provided all the steering information the account manager needed. Post implemented a clearly-structured account-navigating platform which had the necessary tools to handle account teamwork, planning, and performance measurement. The account plans were put into accessible electronic formats. At the same time the company's monthly performance data was made accessible via the dashboard. Rather than the traditional paper sheet or Word document, the account manager was given interactive access to the data at different levels of detail. As a result, any deviation from plans [budget and periodic forecasts] could be tracked down to the level of a specific product or business unit. Performance could be compared to that in a previous period or to comparable customers. Key performance indicators showed the business status quo. Furthermore the progress of strategic goals and tactical actions were closely monitored. What-if scenarios supported further analysis and helped to create new ideas. In addition the system fed performance data with the account manager's comments into the account plan and delivered electronic monthly reports to the department head and to the board of directors.

The 'account navigator' dashboard had the following information structure:

  - *planning information* — account plans, opportunity plans and budgets and periodic forecasts derived from these account and opportunity plans;

- *control information* — quantitative results [realisation] and qualitative performance information [e.g. progress of strategic goals and planned actions] indicated by the account manager in the management report;
- *steering information* derived from the confrontation of planning and realisation and expressed in the account plans and opportunity plans in which planned actions are described;
- *quantitative planning and realisation information* which could be analysed beyond the borders of one account, supported and displayed by an OLAP [On Line Analytical Processing] environment.

After selecting a specific account in the dashboard, the user can open the active account plan, the campaign or opportunity plans or the most recent management report of this account. These active plans and reports can be updated any time. The system can print out whole plans, or chapters, or even smaller parts of the plans and reports. It retrieves quantitative information regarding products, accounts, account managers, etc. In addition to this interactive retrieval of information it can zoom in and out and 'turn over' the database to get a more detailed view on the data from different perspectives. By doing this, the user gains a quicker and deeper understanding of these data. The account manager may also record personal views and save them, to get this information next time by the click of the mouse.

At the highest level, the account navigator is a well-organised hierarchical archive of documents of which the top layer is the account. Every user can define a personal dashboard to obtain further analyses, what-if scenarios and navigation through the available data.
Post equipped their customer leaders with the 'account navigator' system. Using it, the organisation now gets an improved and accurate view on all accounts. Account team members are able to pursue and report on defined actions in a clearly structured way. New information concerning the accounts is updated constantly and saved for the company [not only in the heads of the account managers]. The account manager

gets rapid knowledge of deviations in realisation versus planning.

From a conceptual viewpoint, the navigator system is an advanced and useful tool to manage the customer relationship on a direct and ongoing basis. One of the important next steps to be taken must be a more strategic use of the relevant data on specific, individual customers, data squeezed from the factory's operational processes. Specific data on the customers' traffic flows can be the basis of real 'value-selling'.

4.7.3 Manage the customer-specific value chain

Many large organisations have post box numbers. Mail from anywhere in the country is collected and delivered to this one address. What more could Post do to provide further value?

While delivery of the mail to the post box is reliable, there are subsequent delays of, at times, a week before the mail arrives at the desk of the person within the recipient organisation. How can Post anticipate this and deliver mail rapidly to the recipient? Or should it just enter into competition with the customer's mailroom? For that matter, who is the customer in this situation? The post box holder does not pay for the stamp, the senders do!

Let us examine the information that the postal organisation has – and can have – in co-operation with the customer. Post knows who sends mail to the post box holder. It also knows where it comes from. This knowledge could determine where processing should best take place. If Post can use sophisticated character recognition technology to recognise the sender's name, it can match the sender data with the internal organisation of the addressee company. As a result, Post can then deliver the mail directly to the people who are responsible for handling that specific mail [for example, an insurance claim sent by the policy holder to the insurance company post box].

The forward integration of the postal processes with those of its main customers is an opportunity. Post could do print-and-mail, directly linking computer output to postal processes. It could print and deliver e-mail, and so forth. Post could also open the envelope, scan its contents, and send them electronically to the addressee, saving the box-holder many paper-handling tasks.

The example of the post-box customer suggests that Post must do more than deliver from one address to the other. At the point of entry of the mail into the postal system, Post must know the intended recipient and how best to facilitate its delivery to that named person. Thus it can derive new value from the recipient as well as from the sender. In this way Post accelerates the physical, electronic or hybrid mail processes of sender and receiver. The overall cost of these processes is less, and Post has improved the overall efficiency of the mailing process! This is integral management of the value chain from sender to recipient.

Integral management of the postal chain requires full customer-specific management of the postal processes from anywhere in the system at any time. Today, a unique code is printed on every envelope that is the 'run code' for the sorting process. This data can also be used as a 'data link' to the customer processes.

In practice these thought processes concerning the customer-specific management of factory processes have only just begun. It is still difficult to see how the seeming contradictions of customised processes and mass production can be reconciled without losing benefits of scale. The courier companies have taken a lead on the necessary informational management of their processes. For example, FedEx provides tracing data on individual parcels via the Internet. It gives the time of arrival, the sender data, and much more. This can generate new sources of revenue such as recipient-defined delivery times, redirecting a parcel to another destination while on route, or direct delivery to stock points. However, Fedex must then allow its customer to 'interfere' with the ongoing transportation process.

4.7.4   Design the service encounter

A second aspect of postal value chain management concerns the customers' interface with the service entry points: the post box on the corner of the street, the post office, business counters, mailbag collectors, call centres, the Internet, and so forth. Post must see every service entry point as a chance to increase the value of service contact.

When you send a parcel at the business counter of Canadian Post, they will 'help' you to find the best way of sending it. They will ask: "Where is it going? When do you want it to arrive? Are you aware of the customs regulations in that country; shall we arrange the necessary papers? May I suggest that you take out insurance on this? Do you want us to take cash on delivery?"

A computer screen – the customer dashboard – guides the counter personnel and the customer through the intake or booking process. Software-defined processes inform the insurance company that the customer has taken out insurance. The customer's identity is checked: do they have an account, do they have privilege status? What do we know about the customer's usual mail requirements? The customer can use the same applications for 'self-service', ordering postal services from his or her desk. The postal organisation has redesigned its service delivery points.

As it did in the example of the mail order company, Post will rely on digital business technologies to support its customers in their full communications processes with their own customers. The mail order company may wish to outsource many of the physical handling aspects of its business, from distributing catalogues and physical goods to the invoicing and collection systems. However, the mail order company will always want to have information control over customer contact points held by third parties such as Post. To work with this control, Post must develop a very deep understanding of its customers' business and develop the tools and command systems for customer-specific management of its production systems.

4.7.5   Lessons for Total Action

The simple act of sending an envelope or package from one person to another invokes a complex delivery chain which most postal administrations now manage with high effectiveness. Mail would appear to be a 'commodity' which, given the advent of competition, might be emulated. In fact, it can be transformed into high value services for both the sender and recipient of the mail. To achieve this Post had to develop a new relationship with its largest customers, using customer leaders and customer action teams. These faced the challenge of developing an entirely new understanding of Post through the eyes of the customer. Moreover, to ensure that customer leaders were equipped to lead with the customer, Post had to put customer dashboards in place to provide essential information.

The process of engaging outside-in was paramount in developing the skills of the customer leaders and their teams and, as important, to ensure the co-operation and linking of Post's operational chimneys.

The postman calls twice, both on sender and on recipient. Digital business technologies allowed Post to take significant advantage from this customer-to-customer communications platform, with the application of Total Action principles.

5   Engaging outside-in:
the route to Total Action

There is only one starting point for Total Action: the customer. Fatal Inaction is characterised by failure at the interface between the organisation and its customers. The optimal route to Total Action begins with discovery – or rediscovery – of the customer.

To ensure that every activity revolves around and derives from the customer, the organisation must engage outside-in; it must identify and eliminate those activities that are not customer-relevant. This is a question of organising and 'mind setting' – ensuring that everyone understands the 'customer as driver', that everyone believes it, and that everyone is engaged across and into the organisation, so the customer becomes truly the centre of the organisation's universe.

At the same time, as this organisational engagement emerges, the information platforms must be driven into place to enable the near-complete communication Total Action demands. This requires the active participation of the IT department, as well as every other function. You cannot achieve Total Action without harnessing the capabilities of the digital business technologies.

5.1   The challenges of Total Action

The philosophy may be straightforward: Make the customer the locus of decision-making, under the leadership of customer leaders supported by high-quality, well-trained teams of people. These customer action teams will direct the activities of the Total Action organisation and its business partners. Aided by instant information from the customer dashboard, they will manage the commitment and fulfilment processes in an ongoing cycle of seamless communication with the customer and within their – temporary – supply-chains. The traditional back office will become integrated with the front office in a 'fluid, self organising culture' which continually tries to match the company's mission with the immediate opportunities in the market place.

The practice has been different! The obvious truth of 'customer first' is challenged in so many guises:

- It's dangerous to relinquish 'control' to the customer this way.
- We understand the need to link to the customer but, for many of our employees and departments, the individual customer isn't relevant!
- We have numerous 'customer solutions' in place and many organisational initiatives which are, in essence, driving our organisation towards Total Action ... so what are you offering that's new!
- Our employees and our senior management are already bound into a variety of change activities. Are you suggesting that we put additional loads on them?
- We have enough problems trying to bring our IT up to date. IT isn't yet ready to support the potential of your digital business technologies!
- We know that we must do something. We see the internal markets and the growth of corporate autism. But we don't know where to begin! Can you give us a checklist of action points?

The real questions are:

- Why should we do this and why is Total Action different?
- Where – and how – do we begin?
- What next?

5.2   Why should we do this...and what's different?

The advent of digital business technologies is probably the most important driver for this new customer mandate. The increase in interactive capabilities that can result from the effective use of these technologies offers both the opportunity for new success and the threat of visible failure.

The large organisation, in particular, must be aware of the new challenges which the digital business technologies provide. History has shown that even the largest, seemingly the most secure, organisations can fail. Who could ever have thought that IBM would lose billions? Where is the line between confidence and hubris? Many companies, having brought their 'chip of genius' to the marketplace and having managed and survived the dangers of growth, grow secure in their leadership positions and begin to suffer from hubris – that feeling of supreme mastery of their world, without threat. This self-confidence drives the security of the status quo – 'it worked yesterday, so it will work tomorrow' – and also supports the misery of the internal market and the contagion of corporate autism. The effects of this disability to recognise and serve the customer, will be magnified by the new, digital business technologies.

The US military case showed how a huge organisation that had been slipping towards Fatal Inaction, could pull itself together, power through massive internal walls, and use digital business technologies to put information at the front line, literally. Only with the soldier at the front managing the information could they develop pinpoint accuracy. Military leaders recognised that the *technology alone would not be enough*. Others had more or better weapons. The best warfare technology was essential but the *doctrine* had to change: *leadership* had to become as important as firepower, the fighting qualities of soldiers had to be improved so that they acted to their full capacity with a superior war-fighting method. This combination of mindset and technology showed its worth in the Gulf war.

The American Airlines case showed how one organisation pulled together all the information about its own portfolio of services – flights – and then used the technology to create a value chain that could be tapped by the customer leader to fill the customer's requirements. Information, throughout the process, is crucial. The SABRE system helps American Airlines seduce the customer, take the order, and collect payment. Fulfilling the customer's order involves other parties such as airports, customs and immigration, and air traffic control, for which no individual airline can guarantee service levels. However, the airline that can keep passengers informed about delays, new times of departure, etc., may ultimately gain some competitive edge.

First Direct demonstrated that it is the concept rather than the technology that gives the edge. The lowly telephone is the customer's contact, but the banking representative (or customer leader) has all the information on tap to fulfil that customer's requests, both for information and for services. Once again, the empowered front-line gives more accurate targeting for corporate firepower.

The police case demonstrated that the awareness of the customer has to come first, before any application of digital business technologies can improve an organisation's performance. This is true 'discovery'. Until police forces perceive their role in the value chain of security risks, there is no customer. Once they have a clearly defined mission for the customer, the police are able to create customer leaders and customer action teams, with clear customer-centred performance metrics. Only then, by examining the requirements of these teams, can the police decide the information support and the platforms to deliver this support.

The cases demonstrate that acting outside-in – from the customer into the organisation – is a crucial success factor for Total Action. Dell Computer, in making its PC to the individual customer order, gives us a clear example of how organisations can act outside-in. Dell's component manufacturers can identify and relate to the individual customer. They receive an electronic order for the components required and deliver them according to the requirements of the order. These component manufacturers must be integrated into a tightly coupled business network, with strong interactive capabilities to give the customer the best performance. As the customer completes the order, the customer action team forms for that customer event, as Dell communicates information on the customer and the customer goals clearly and unambiguously to every participant.

There are many similar examples of the effective application of the elements and principles of Total Action. Their common denominator is real customer focus and customer-derived actions enabled by the capabilities of digital business technologies. This resulting unification of all activities to make customer interaction a cohesive recognised process that engages the whole organisation is the difference that Total Action brings to ensuring organisational effectiveness.

While Total Action can be regarded as simply an organisational – or management – concept, its difference and its strength lie in the rediscovery of the customer. And, in particular, the engagement of the organisation resulting from the new understandings brought about by this rediscovery. Total Action does not seek to invalidate or displace other concepts, rather it seeks to build on them and solidify their results into measurable performance improvements. These improvements include:

- *change in the organisation's perception of the customer*
  By adopting the Total Action approach, members of the organisation begin to understand that digital business technologies enable them to add more value and improve performance for the customer. Consequently they re-positioned and strengthened their position in the value-chain. The recognition of the customer and the process of creating customer value, particularly in non-commercial organisations such as government departments or the police, have resulted in major shifts in management approach. It also has changed IT priorities, towards a deeper understanding of the organisation's real challenges and priorities. The resulting platforms and systems

support more effectively those with responsibility for serving customers as well as those who seek deeper knowledge of customer behaviour and organisational performance. The identification of new performance metrics has been very important in most organisations. In addition, closing the information distance between the 'back office' – those who must ensure fulfilment – and the front line has been of great value. Consequently, the design and development of forms of the customer dashboard has been the vehicle for delivering this essential support.

– *deeper understanding of the impact of digital business technologies*
The understanding that digital business technologies demand far better co-ordination of their internal management of customer data has been critical. Opening web sites or any other form of customer link cannot help if the organisation is unable to maintain a unified view on the customer nor act on their knowledge of the customer. This is not a technical issue of building the one, large database of all customer data. Nor has it been seen that way. Rather, it has been seen as a management issue: *a question of building intelligence on the customer and then being prepared to act on it.*

– *the key role of customer leader and customer action teams*
Many organisations in some way have adopted and implemented customer leaders and customer action teams. These concepts are not entirely new. Much of the literature on sales and account management reveals the basics of the approach. However, as stated before, such approaches, such as account management, do not succeed without the strong informational and action links to fulfilment. Without these links, the account manager becomes a super-sales person at best, with few tools to find and use essential customer information. In addition, they usually have no mandate to form customer action teams and to drive outside-in methods into the organisation.

– *integral management of the supply chain*

The modular design of business networks as an analytical and implementation approach cannot be understated. Nevertheless, the initial effort of building the raw model for each of the business partners can seem prohibitive. In a number of cases detail process diagrams of intra- and inter-organisational processes have been produced helping organisations to develop alternative, more effective designs for their business partner networks and their internal fulfilment. For them, the key importance of fulfilment became very clear. The issues surrounding fulfilment [uniform definition of essential processes, the sharing of vital transaction data, and common command and control] were clearly identified and addressed. In addition, the first steps in the redefinition of the portfolio in new customer-based terms has produced great value.

– *engaging outside-in*

The most emotional aspects of embedding Total Action have been the intensive 'engaging outside-in' sessions with top executives. These sessions did not so much address the complicated issues around the technology. Rather they opened executive eyes to the inadequacy of current performance and the inability to respond to the simple logic of 'putting the customer first and taking action'. Simultaneously, executives are challenged by the 'business-as-usual' demands of their management for improved earnings. This mindset, and these demands, often resulted in contentious discussions.

Managers were faced with determining new key performance indicators which asked them to measure and improve their value to their: *customers, organisation* and *subordinates* according to the mandate of Total Action: making every activity customer activity.

Outside-in engagement is a critical success factor for the Total Action approach. Directing attention to the customer and performance for the customer quickly reveals significant gaps in individual and organisational knowledge, understanding, and capabilities. The two simple questions: *who is the 'customer' you serve?* and *how well do you serve this customer?* have been the starting point for many of the authors' Total Action experiences.

There is only one starting point for Total action: the customer!

5.3   Where – and how – do we begin?

Many managers, on behalf of their organisations, can ask the wrong questions. They are reacting to changes in the weather, rather than the climate, or identifying specific failures in specific parts of their organisations rather than seeing the underlying reasons for failures in performance. In many of these cases, the lack of strong direct linkages to the customer and, as a result, the inability to act for the customer, underpins their dilemmas.

Again, the two questions: *who is the 'customer' you serve?* and *how well do you serve this customer?* opened up the discussions to reveal that, indeed, the Total Action approach of outside-in engagement had to be the starting point for moving to performance improvements.

Asking these questions at the sales front or most top management can bring some sharp answers. However, when asking these questions deep in the bowels of the organisation – the IT department, product development, or strategic and business planning – the answers become more vague. Even in sales support organisations, the 'customer distance' can be very large.

The essence of the Total Action approach is to engage the organisation. From the starting point of the customer – this engagement follows three distinct steps: *rediscover the customer, revitalise the relationship* and *renewal.*

Step One — discover the customer

Reverse the traditional dependency: 'my customer needs me' into 'I need my customer, therefore I must discover and understand my customer' is the new logic. By forming *customer action teams* mandated

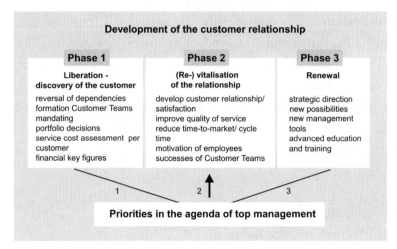

Fig. 5.1. Steps to Total Action

to discover the reality of specific customers, the organisation can determine:

– the true state of the customer's dependence;
– the organisation's dependence on the customer; and
– how to create wholesome customer dependence through the delivery of real value.

This demands that *performance with the customer* is understood and measured, so new *performance metrics* can be designed, which truly reflect the value that must be delivered. Performance metrics must also include financial metrics including, for example, a service cost assessment for each customer.

As a result, essential *portfolio decisions* have to be taken to define the capabilities which:

– are needed by the customer;
– are not yet recognised by the customer; and
– we [and our business network] *can* and *must* deliver?

Step two — revitalise the relationship

While establishing the customer dependencies and performance metrics, the relationship with the customer must be revitalised. Establishing customer leaders and customer action teams for selected customers can be a strong starting point. These individuals and teams rediscover the customer, while determining the critical actions which must be taken to re-establish credibility with that customer. These actions often include:

- improving quality of service;
- adhering to performance metrics;
- seeking to reduce 'time-to-market' while beginning to understand and enact proactive 'market-to-time' solutions; and
- motivating people through their engagement with the customer action teams.

Step three — renewal

Renewal is an ongoing process. At this stage it means absorbing the operational capabilities into the new strategic directions of Total Action. This includes:

- acting rapidly on the new possibilities which have been identified and translating them into customer satisfaction;
- defining the win-win partnership which both sides desire; and
- planting advanced education and training into the organisation and across the business to continue and develop the engagement which has been created.

Engaging outside-in

Total Action begins with *engaging outside-in*. This requires that the *atoms of service* for the customer are determined for all contact points and are driven deep into those parts of the organisations that must deliver. No organisation can change its behaviour overnight although many seem to have tried. Working outside-in means:

- determining what is important to the customer – the value to the customer;
- identifying how this 'value' will be delivered [the customer contact points and portfolio of capabilities];
- putting in place clearly-defined and agreed metrics for performance with the customer; and
- driving *customer obsession* deep into the organisation so everyone understands the value which they deliver, as individuals and teams.

The digital business technologies must be mastered and put in place to increase interactive capabilities so that true working outside-in is achieved.

There is, perhaps, no finer challenge than engaging the 'IT organisation' and seeking to ensure that it operates according to the mandates of Total Action. Wherever one begins the Total Action initiative, one must confront the capabilities of the IT organisations. These organisations, in most cases, have the mandate to deliver the digital business technologies: the information and communication platforms that ensure external and internal productivity.

5.4   Mindset over matter

Technology can keep Total Action from happening, but it can't make it happen. Only human beings, wanting to win, can do that. So the most important message for those who would like to move towards Total Action is to get the mindset right. First the mindset of the people inside the organisation and in its value chain – and then the people in customer organisations who begin to appreciate the new focus.

Information requirements are decided by the mindset

When you are caught speeding, the police officer needs different information than that needed if you were injured in a car crash. In the case of speeding the officer must be able to check your motoring records and the records of your car. That done, the officer can decide, out of a pattern of set alternatives, which action to take. The intended application of the information is clear-cut.

Suppose you were injured in a car crash. The first duty of the police would be to organise assistance. Immediate reference to your medical records would be very helpful. To get at this information the policeman would need instant real time access to your doctor or hospital. The ambulance, already on its way to the scene, would receive this information. Meanwhile the officer would need to arrange clear passage for the ambulance and manage the other traffic. A doctor, using the police communication system, could give the relevant instructions in first aid to the police person on the scene.

Make the person at the front line the director of events

If you are caught speeding, all the police officer has to do is to fine you. In your hypothetical car crash the officer must act very differently. In today's world, if the police contacted the hospital, it would probably not transmit your medical records.

Nothing could be done until doctors arrived at the scene of the accident. Time would be lost which might cost you your life! Prior decisions about who should have received which information would have wasted time. The officer could not become a real director of overall operations because their is no instant access to remote databases.

If the police did have such access, the victim of a road accident could be identified more quickly. The correct actions could be rapidly determined. The police officer could become an effective organiser of help and direct the hospital, ambulance, doctor, traffic management, car removal, and insurance arrangements.

Sadly, in real life, this is not the case. The police mindset has pre-scribed the officer's information requirements. The police officer does not, and as things are, cannot, act as the 'director of events'. The victim of a car accident is not seen as a 'customer' and the officer does not act as a 'customer liaison officer'. A fundamental rethink of the essence of police work is required if such attitudes are to become current.

Similar anomalies exist in many other mindsets. Recall the American Airlines case. Is the airline business about flying planes around the globe with the incidental boarding of passengers to pay for flying them? Or is it about getting a person comfortably from one place to another within an agreed period of time? Is police work about law enforcement? Or is it about creating a secure environment to work and live for the law-abiding citizen?

This mindset about where and how information is applied – what is the locus of decision-making – is the key to making sure information can be used effectively at the point of customer contact. Necessary information must be organised so it can easily be linked to all sorts of seemingly unrelated events. Too often as a result of 'data museums', however, information is simply not accessible, even when it is available. To succeed, data must be captured and managed quite independent to the functionality of the system. Data must also be captured in such a way that it is easily connectable to other systems so that it can be re-used instantly.

The Internet has shown the way. With hyperlinks and the World Wide Web, the end user decides which information to collect, organise and link. Intelligent software agents can seek out information on demand. This intelligent information linking is the cornerstone for organising future customer information. It is, however, very distant from the traditional mindsets of traditional IT people.

The mindset of the customer can affect an organisation's success or failure. Levitt wrote about 'product surround', which affects the mindset of the customer:

> 'We live in an age in which our thinking about what a product or service is must be quite different from what it was before. It is not so much the basic, generic, central thing which we are thinking

about that counts, but the whole cluster of satisfactions with which we surround it.'[1]

Lovelock[2] concentrated on the importance of *core* and *supplementary* services, noting that while a company usually concentrates on its core services, the competitive advantage usually comes with high performance on the *supplementary* service elements. Hence Virgin Airlines could focus on the tiny TV at each seat, while coping with the problems of learning to run an airline. *Performance* – the quality and value of the result that is delivered to the recipient – is critical. This performance involves the measured quality of both the core product and its product surround.

The core product is a measurable and tangible deliverable. For the airline it is the aircraft seat you booked – combined with taking-off and landing at the agreed time with your luggage returned to you when you arrive at your destination airport. The core product must perform to the specification promised.

For an express parcel service the core product is picking up a package when and where agreed and delivered to the agreed address at the agreed time. If the company does not perform on this core product then it will not survive. Lovelock points out that core products tend to become commodities with increasing competition. Therefore, it is necessary to compete on the basis of more than the product surround. The product surround clothes the core product in attributes which can set it apart from the competition. Attributes of product surround include:

- *make the product easy to buy* through setting it in a convenient and attractive context;
- *make it easy to use* by providing clear, necessary information, and
- *make it easy to keep* by providing strong after-sales support.

Remember the example of the service engineer non-visit. In this case after-sales support, although contracted, failed. As we struggle through our ordinary days, we are continually confronted by such examples of service failure. They may be trivial [the airline is not carrying the newspaper I always read], annoying [the ticket office does not tell you that the train for which you are buying a ticket is not running] or almost catastrophic [we have no record of your hotel reservation]. However, they seem commonplace even when dealing with some of the so-called, customer-attentive world-leading companies. Usually it is not the product failure itself which angers. It is the lack of information about that failure which incites one to move to a new supplier.

All customer encounters and experiences are an accumulation of those 'atoms' of service which combine to reveal the true portfolio of capabilities of the delivering organisation. The dividing line between product surround and the core product can be indistinct. It may be unwise to attempt to define an absolute distinction between them. There is always the danger that the surround becomes viewed as an expensive extra, rather than something which is ingrained in the commitment to the customer.

The dividing line between the two, if it exists, certainly moves. American Airlines, with SABRE and AAdvantage, moved the borderline between the core product of 'flying a passenger' and the additional services which were provided. As soon as an airline introduced boarding cards with seat allocations the need for the 50 metre sprint to the seat disappeared. From that point on, an airline on the same route without boarding cards would be at a disadvantage [unless they were competing on rock-bottom prices].

Five years ago, you did not expect a fully itemised bill from the telephone company. It was unheard of. You got what you expected and were satisfied. You were delighted when the company introduced itemised billing. What you got exceeded your expectations – for a while. However, six months later the 'get' equalled the 'expect' since the itemised bill was then standard. If you then worked in another country where you didn't get itemised billing, you were dissatisfied, and suspicious of the service and technical prowess of the operator.

This is where the Total Action concentration on the customer as the source of performance improvement and innovation is vital. We must be able to construct and deliver clearly differentiable services by the use of the information we have squeezed from the individual and similar customers.

There are three key components of the service relationship with the customer:

- *the tangible elements* — those which the customer actually receives; and
- *the behaviour of people* — the customer's experience in dealing with staff; and
- *the processes* — the systems and procedures which deliver service to the customer and support staff in their dealings with the customer.

Give the customer excellent interaction

Excellence in customer interaction demands that close attention be paid to all customer contacts, no matter what the access channel, since these will define the customer's perception of your business competence and lay the foundations of their business relationship with you.

The people or systems interacting with the customer must be supported effectively by the back office. The information infrastructure must be organised to deliver what is required at the front-line. This involves: managing the format, content and goals of the interaction and determining how to fulfil the results of the interaction.

When a customer or potential customer initiates or responds to an interaction they can have a variety of goals. In the majority of interactions a customer is seeking information, making a complaint, or seeking to solve a problem. All customers' goals differ.

Excellence in customer interaction

General Electric's inquiry centre receives 2 million calls each year, of which only 10% are complaints; the remainder are sales leads. And when customers complain and are dealt with professionally GE has a 95% chance that the customer will repurchase the product.

From the customer's viewpoint excellence of interaction can be measured in terms of:

- *time — rapid access and speed of response*
  The customer's ability to access the appropriate person or information within an acceptable time span together with the speed of the company's response to the goals of the interaction;
- *value — the relevance/value of the response*
  The interaction meets the customer's requirements and the information provided is relevant, accurate and clear; and
- *simplicity —* unnecessary complexity is removed from communication.

In other words, from the supplier's viewpoint, to assure that excellent interaction you need:

- *simplicity of the business relationship* [business instruments, contracts, ordering, complaints handling]; and
- *quality of information* [product descriptions, response to queries, questions, and problems].

Information is a vital component of the interaction. The majority of complaints, it is reported, result from a lack of information about a failure rather than being about the failure itself. In addition, the appropriate information brings the ability to co-ordinate the essential internal resources in order the customer requirements be understood and met.

Ensure access to customer information

Information in today's business environment is becoming more ephemeral than in any time in the past. The field soldier in Napoleon's army had few information requirements compared with the soldiers who served the Gulf. The modern soldier requires a great deal of real-time information. As with the soldier, the requirement for business information has become increasingly unpredictable. Location and situation will determine the specific information which is needed:

- *Location* — where the information is needed. Access to the information must be organised from any point where it will be needed.
- *Situation* — the intended use, or application, of the information.

Today's focus on customer data is intense. Whether it be a supermarket chain, or an airline seeking to ensure customer loyalty, or an industrial company using account management to derive knowledge of their customers to build their business, they demand huge quantities of information. These organisations are making, or at least trying to make, 'data mines': advanced computer database systems containing as much information on the customer as possible.

These huge and costly projects too often turn into a nightmare when they fail to deliver. The pay back is sometime hence; the up-front investment large. The risk of failure is high, since, being so large, these projects are vulnerable to technical and organisational problems. Rethinking the essential customer information becomes critical to the success of such projects.

What information would you, as a sales person, account manager, or business leader, really need? There are three components to essential customer information:

– *The invariant customer data* — the singular identity of the customer
This is not just a matter of name/ address/ numbers, or generalised
customer data. You have to be able to 'recognise' a customer from
a range of operational data.

For example, if you are a postal business, the sender is a customer
[the one who pays], but the recipient is often the source of the
value of the service. The post office must capture the data on who
sends what to whom, when, and why. This is the basis for
individualising the service and deriving more business through,
for instance, tracking and tracing or redirecting incoming mail in
real time for recipients.

Too often a postal service is regarded as being of value only to the
sender. When you have ordered a book from the digital bookshop,
it is a value to you to know that it has been shipped. Or to know
where it is and have the ability to re-route the book as it moves
towards you.

– *Performance data on the individual customer*
How well do you, as an organisation, perform for each specific
customer? Traditional performance criteria are:
- financial -turnover;
- margin;
- share of customer business;
- customer satisfaction;
- employee motivation; and
- innovative strength.

Whichever criteria are chosen, they must be a clear translation of
your company's mission into what is important for the specific
customer. You need reliable and non-disputed figures which relate
uniquely to that identified customer.

– *Development over time*

You need to access historical data, to build knowledge of the customer, and of your performance, and to differentiate services to 'care for the customer'. This dimension in time also concerns to the future action and performance targets you set for yourself for individual customers as part of your customer action planning.

The starting point is to take decisions on the *template of information* essential for customer action. Imagine that you have all the customer-specific information possible:

– what could this mean?
– what would you do differently and what would the benefits be, to you, and to the customer?
– what information do you really need?
– where is it today – inside, outside, with the customer, in the actions of the customer?
– how would you obtain this information?
– what is the cost, time and resource needed to obtain it?

There is no simple 'checklist' for this template. It must be clearly determined for your chosen customer groups or individual customers and be linked, through your portfolio, to your capabilities and mission. It is not a matter of determining competencies. The customer information template must bring together the performance and behavioural data which are, and will be, important to your organisation and the customer. The portfolio matrix and the concepts of account management and customer leadership provide the tools for building the template. The customer dashboard provides for the 'presentation' of the template with the sales front.

To achieve this, the desired information must be mined to fill the template with real and reliable customer data. There must be a 'data sheet' or 'home page' for every customer. Using today's technology –

groupware, intranet – data elements can be inter-linked and it is possible to navigate through this information. The collection of all customer data sheets forms the market intelligence of the company.

5.5 What next?

Convinced of the need for Total Action, you, as a manager, call a meeting of your peers: managers from the front-line to the back office and your organisations 'factory'. The agenda is straightforward: *'over two hours I wish to identify'*:

- who is our 'customer';
- how well we perform for this 'customer'; and
- whether we are really using the capabilities of digital business technologies.

Prepare your Total Action presentation: twenty minutes on the need for and the ingredients of Total Action. Then force the discussion into the depth of these questions. Open the eyes. Trigger intellectual and operational engagement. Set the goals and the timelines. Start making it work.

It is relatively straightforward to determine your own score on Total Action using the Total Action scorecard. It requires that you draw on the experiences and knowledge of your own organisation, particularly the front line, and those of your customers. A good impression of how well your technical infrastructure is being used in comparison with that of your competitors and other industries can be gained relatively quickly and form the basis of a rigorous evaluation.

There is no generic recipe or checklist for assessing your position and the steps that you must take. But, we hope, this book gives you the pointers and the direction. At the heart is general agreement that something must be and can be done – the motivation of change. The responsibility for this must lie with you, management!

* **Notes**

1 The boardroom agenda

1. Levitt, T. [1969], *Marketing for Business Growth*, McGraw-Hill, New York

2. Magretta, J. [1998], *The Power of Virtual Integration: An Interview with Dell Computer's Michael Dell*, Harvard Business Review, March-April 1998, pp. 73-84

3. www.amazon.com

4. Attributed to Keith More, Planning and Media Manager, Abbey National Bank.

5. This was the real life situation at Tesco (UK) where they offered Internet grocery shopping in 1998.

6. Juran, J.M. [1964], *Managerial breakthrough*, McGraw-Hill, New York

7. Crosby, P.B. [1984], *Quality is free*, McGraw-Hill, New York

2 Digital business technologies and Total Action

1. www.amazon.com

2. www.dell.com

3. Business Week Online, September 10, 1998

4. Press report of a survey of UK financial institutions, 1997

5. The Sunday Times, February 1, 1998, *'Tesco hi-tech shoppers log into old world'*

6. See for instance Brynjolfsson, E. [1993], *The productivity paradox of information technology*, Communications of the ACM, 36, 12, pp. 67-77

7. Hopper, M.D. [1990], *Rattling SABRE - new ways to compete on information*, Harvard Business Review, May-June 1990, pp. 118-125

8. Both cases are resported extensively in business publications.

9. Keen, P.W.G. [1986], *Competing in time - Using Telecommunications for Competitive Advantage*, Ballinger Publishing Company

10. Benjamin, R.I., D.W. de Long, M.S. Scott Morton [1990], *Electronic Data Interchange: How Much Competitive Advantage?*, Long Range Planning, 23, 1, pp. 29-40

11. Forrester Research, reported in Business Week, July 1998

12. Business Week, European Edition, September 7, 1998, pp. 41 - 48

13. 'Jerry's Guide to the World Wide Web".

14. Peppers, D., M. Rogers [1997], *Enterprise One to One: Tools for Competing in the Interactive Age*, Doubleday, New York

15. Porter, M.E. [1980], *Competitive strategy*, Free Press, New York

16. Vervest, P.H.M. [1994], *Communication, not information: an ad-hoc organisation of the value chain*, Inaugural Speech, Erasmus University Rotterdam, The Netherlands

17. Hoogeweegen, M.R. [1997], *Modular Network Design: Assessing the Impact of EDI*, Dissertation, Erasmus University Rotterdam

18. ibid 16

19. Baldwin, C.Y., K.B. Clark [1997], *Managing in an Age of Modularity*, Harvard Business Review, September-October 1997, pp. 84-93

20. See for an interesting application of Modular (Business) Network Design in the air cargo industry: Hoogeweegen, M.R., P.H.M. Vervest [1998], *Modularity: Being Agile and Versatile at the Same Time*, Agility & Global Competition, 2, 4, pp. 23-34

3   Weeding out Fatal Inaction

1. Reichheld, F.F. [1996], *Learning from Customer Defections*, Harvard Business Review, March-April 1996

2. Fayol, F.W. [1916], *Administration Industrielle et Generale*, Dunod, Paris

3. Taylor, F.W. [1911], *The Principles of Scientific Management*, Harper & Row, New York

4. Lussato, B. [1976], *A critical introduction to organisation theory*

5. Huczynski A and Buchanan D [1997], *Organisational Behaviour*, Prentice Hall Europe

6. Mouzelis, N.P. [1968], *Organisation and Bureaucracy: an Analysis of Modern Theories*, Walter De Gruyter

7. Burns, T., G.M. Stalker [1961], *The Management of Innovation*, Tavistock, London

8. Kanter, R.M. [1985], *Change Masters: Innovation for Productivity in the American Corporation*, Simon & Schuster, New York

9. Levitt, T. [1969], *Marketing for Business Growth*, McGraw-Hill, New York

10. Huczynski A and Buchanan D [1997], *Organisational Behaviour*, Prentice Hall Europe

11. Parkinson, C.N. [1957], *Parkinson's Law or the Pursuit of Progress*, Penguin Books, New York

12. Peter, L.J., R. Hull [1969], *The Peter Principle*, William Morrow & Co., Great Britain

13. Adams, S. [1996], *The Dilbert Principle*, HarperCollins, New York

14. based on discussions with Thomas Weesing

15. Sachs, O. [1985], *The Man Who Mistook His Wife for a Hat*, Gerald Duckworth & Co., Great Britain

16. Braverman, H. [1974], *Labour and Monopoly Capital: The Degradation of Work in the Twentieth Century*, Monthly Review Press, New York

17 Matsushita, K. [1993] and Seleznik, A, *Learning Leadership: Cases and Commentaries on Abuses of Power in Organizations*. See also: Matsushita, K [1994], *Not for bread alone,* Berkley Publishing Group

18 Foy, N. [1994], *Empowering People at Work*, Ashgate Publishing Company

4   The Total Action casebook

1. This case has been based on: Pascale, R.T., E.R. Guthrie [1994], *The United States Army: Change or Transformation*, Working Paper. We apologize for not having been able to contact authors and obtain their permission, in sofar as required, but felt the case is too important to omit.

2. ibid

3. Hopper, M.D. [1990], *Rattling SABRE — new ways to compete on information*, Harvard Business Review, May-June 1990, pp. 118-125

4. www.travelocity.com

5. Heller, J. [1965], *Catch 22*, Dell Publishing

6. Steiner, T.D., D.B. Teixeira [1990], *Technology in Banking: Creating Value and Detroying Profits*, Irwin Professional Publishing

7. www.firstdirect.co.uk

8. Attributed to Mike Siddons

9. Attributed to Rob Hessing, Chief of Police, Rotterdam, 1996

5   Engaging outside–in: the route to total Action

1. Levitt, T. [1969], *Marketing for Business Growth*, McGraw-Hill, New York, p. 74

2. Lovelock, C.H. [1994], *Product Plus: How Product + Service = Competitive Advantage*, McGraw-Hill

★ **Bibliography**

Adams, S. [1996], *The Dilbert Principle*, HarperCollins, New York

Baldwin, C.Y., K.B. Clark [1997], *Managing in an Age of Modularity*, Harvard Business Review, September-October 1997, pp. 84–93

Benjamin, R.I., D.W. de Long, M.S. Scott Morton [1990], *Electronic Data Interchange: How Much Competitive Advantage?*, Long Range Planning, 23, 1, pp. 29-40

Braverman, H. [1974], *Labour and Monopoly Capital: The Degradation of Work in the Twentieth Century*, Monthly Review Press, New York

Brynjolfsson, E. [1993], *The productivity paradox of information technology*, Communications of the ACM, 36, 12, pp. 67-77

Burns, T., G.M. Stalker [1961], *The Management of Innovation*, Tavistock, London

Fayol, F.W. [1916], *Administration Industrielle et Generale*, Dunod, Paris

Foy, N. [1994], *Empowering People at Work*, Ashgate Publishing Company

Heller, J. [1965], *Catch 22*, Dell Publishing

Hoogeweegen, M.R. [1997], *Modular Network Design: Assessing the Impact of EDI*, Dissertation, Erasmus University Rotterdam

Hoogeweegen, M.R., P.H.M. Vervest [1998], *Modularity: Being Agile and Versatile at the Same Time*, Agility & Global Competition, 2, 4, pp. 23-34

Hopper, M.D. [1990], *Rattling SABRE - new ways to compete on information*, Harvard Business Review, May-June 1990, pp. 118-125

Huczynski A and Buchanan D [1997], *Organisational Behaviour*, Prentice Hall Europe

Kanter, R.M. [1985], *Change Masters: Innovation for Productivity in the American Corporation*, Simon & Schuster, New York

Keen, P.W.G. [1986], *Competing in time - Using Telecommunications for Competitive Advantage*, Ballinger Publishing Company

Levitt, T. [1969], *Marketing for Business Growth*, McGraw-Hill, New York

Lovelock, C.H. [1994], *Product Plus: How Product + Service = Competitive Advantage*, McGraw-Hill

Lussato, B. [1976], *A critical introduction to organisation theory*

Magretta, J. [1998], *The Power of Virtual Integration: An Interview with Dell Computer's Michael Dell*, Harvard Business Review, March-April 1998, pp. 73-84

Matsushita, K. [1993], *Learning Leadership: Cases and Commentaries on Abuses of Power in Organizations*

Mouzelis, N.P. [1968], *Organisation and Bureaucracy: an Analysis of Modern Theories*, Walter De Gruyter

Parkinson, C.N. [1957], *Parkinson's Law or the Pursuit of Progress*, Penguin Books, New York

Pascale, R.T., E.R. Guthrie [1994], *The United States Army: Change or Transformation*, Working Paper

Peppers, D., M. Rogers [1997], *Enterprise One to One: Tools for Competing in the Interactive Age*, Doubleday, New York

Peter, L.J., R. Hull [1969], *The Peter Principle*, William Morrow & Co., Great Britain

Porter, M.E. [1980], *Competitive strategy*, Free Press, New York

Reichheld, F.F. [1996], *Learning from Customer Defections*, Harvard Business Review, March-April 1996

Sachs, O. [1985], *The Man Who Mistook His Wife for a Hat*, Gerald Duckworth & Co., Great Britain

Steiner, T.D., D.B. Teixeira [1990], *Technology in Banking: Creating Value and Detroying Profits*, Irwin Professional Publishing

Taylor, F.W. [1911], *The Principles of Scientific Management*, Harper & Row, New York

Vervest, P.H.M. [1994], *Communication, not information: an ad-hoc organisation of the value chain*, Inaugural Speech, Erasmus University Rotterdam, The Netherlands

Index

★ About the authors

In 1990, Peter Vervest and Al Dunn established *Multimedia Skills*, an innovative telecommunications consultancy and project management company based in London. They were intrigued by the power of the

Professor Peter Vervest

Al Dunn

new digital technologies and amazed about the inability of so many organisations to apply them effectively. As a former Divisional Director of Philips Electronics UK, Peter Vervest (1955) was a real believer in the business benefits of the emerging technologies. Al Dunn (1945) had spent the previous ten years analysing telecommunications and information technology markets working with, amongst others, the Yankee Group Europe delivering multi-client research and, as result, discovering the worlds of the 'customer' – or 'victim'.

Together, they understood that the digital business technologies – which play a pivotal role in this book – can be a great source of innovative advantage. However, to realise this advantage, organisations had to develop entirely new ways to think about and serve their customers. In many assignments, across Europe and in the Pacific Rim, Peter and Al have delivered *'Total Action'* for telecommunications operators, financial institutes, manufacturers, logistics companies, government agencies and others. This developed their experiences in changing organisations 'outside-in': beginning with the customer at the sharp end of the organisation and then driving the challenge of the customer deep inside of, often autistic, corporates. They share their experiences and concepts with you in this book.

Since 1993 Peter Vervest is also Professor of Telecommunications at the Erasmus University Rotterdam, The Netherlands. Both authors travel extensively – to work with their customers. Both are accomplished speakers enthusing many audiences with their succinct views. These centre on what organisations must do in the interconnected world of digital business technologies to ease organisational – and customer – pain.

A.-W. Scheer

ARIS - Business Process Frameworks

ARIS (Architecture of Integrated Information Systems) is a unique and internationally renowned method for optimizing business processes and implementing application systems. This book enhances the proven ARIS concept by describing product flows and explaining how to classify modern software concepts. The importance of the link between business process organization and strategic management is stressed. Bridging the gap between the different approaches in business theory and information technology, the ARIS concept provides a full-circle approach - from the organizational design of business processes to IT implementation. Featuring SAP R/3 as well, real-world examples of various standard software solutions illustrate these concepts.

2nd completely rev. and enlarged ed. 1998.
XVII, 186 pp. 94 figs. Hardcover
*DM 79 / £ 30.50 / FF 298 / Lit. 87.250
ISBN 3-540-64439-3

A.-W. Scheer

ARIS - Business Process Modeling

This book describes in detail how ARIS methods model and realize business processes by means of UML (Unified Modeling Language), leading to an information model that is the keystone for a systematic and intelligent method of developing application systems. Multiple real-world examples - including knowledge management, implementation of workflow systems and standard software solutions (SAP R/3 in particular) - address the deployment of ARIS methods.

2nd completely rev. and enlarged ed. 1999.
XIX, 218 pp. 179 figs.
Hardcover *DM 89 / £ 34 / FF 336 / Lit. 98.290
ISBN 3-540-64438-5

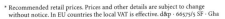

Please order from · Springer GmbH & Co. Customer Service
Haberstr. 7 · D - 69126 Heidelberg, Germany
Tel.: +49 6221 345 200 · Fax: +49 6221 300 186
e-mail: orders@springer.de
or through your bookseller

* Recommended retail prices. Prices and other details are subject to change
without notice. In EU countries the local VAT is effective. d&p · 66575/5 SF · Gha

Springer

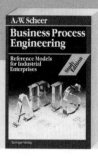

A.-W. Scheer

Business Process Engineering

Reference Models for Industrial Enterprises

The structure of the book follows the business processes of logistics, product development, information and coordination, and offers detailed examples of how outdated organizational structures can be reengineered. Examples from standard software systems (especially SAP R/3) demonstrate the book's down-to-earth practicality. The book develops in the views of the proven „Architecture of Integrated Information Systems" (ARIS) a comprehensive enterprise model, which serves as a reference model for engineering concrete business processes in industrial enterprises.

2nd, completely rev. and enlarged ed. 1994.
XXIV, 770 pp. 580 figs., 26 in colour
Hardcover *DM 128 / £ 49.50 / FF 483 / Lit. 141.360
ISBN 3-540-58234-7

W. Scheer

Business Process Engineering Study Edition

Reference Models for Industrial Enterprises

1998. XXII, 757 pp. 554 figs.
Softcover *DM 75 / £ 29 / FF 283 / Lit. 82.820
ISBN 3-540-63867-9

M. Kirchmer

Business Process Oriented Implementation of Standard Software

How to Achieve Competitive Advantage Efficiently and Effectively

A complete description of a business driven implementation of standard software packages, accelerated by the use of reference models and other information models. The use of those models ensures best quality results and speeds up the software implementation. The book discusses how companies can optimize business processes and realize strategic goals with the implementation of software like SAP R/3, Oracle, Baan or Peoplesoft. It also includes the post implementation activities. The book cites numerous case studies and outlines each step of a process oriented implementation, including the goals, procedures and necessary methods and tools.

2nd ed. 1999. XII, 234 pp. 107 figs.
Hardcover *DM 98 / £ 37.50 / FF 370 / Lit. 108.230
ISBN 3-540-65575-1

Please order from · Springer GmbH & Co. Customer Service
Haberstr. 7 · D - 69126 Heidelberg, Germany
Tel.: +49 6221 345 200 · Fax: +49 6221 300 186
e-mail: orders@springer.de
or through your bookseller

* Recommended retail prices. Prices and other details are subject to change
without notice. In EU countries the local VAT is effective. d&p · 66575/1 SF · Gha

H. Österle, E. Fleisch, R. Alt (Eds.)

Business Networking

Shaping Enterprise Relationships
on the Internet

Electronic commerce, supply chain management, customer relationship management, and other forms of Business Networking will fundamentally change the way business will be conducted in the information age. We will see close collaboration between processes of different enterprises, and above all, new enterprises and new processes. Business Networking offers exceptional opportunities for innovators and harbors fundamental risks for slowpokes. This book proposes a process-oriented model for Business Networking and the concept of networkability to develop realistic strategies for managing enterprises relationships in the Internet economy. It formulates key success factors and management guidelines which were developed in close cooperation between research and practice.

1999. XVI, 376 pp. 109 figs., 39 tabs.
Hardcover *DM 98 / £ 37.50 / FF 370 /
Lit. 108.230
ISBN 3-540-66612-5

**M. Shaw, R. Blanning, T. Strader,
A. Whinston** (Eds.)

Handbook on Electronic Commerce

The world is undergoing a revolution to a digital economy, with pronounced implications for corporate strategy, marketing, operations, information systems, customer services, global supply-chain management, and product distribution. This handbook examines the aspects of electronic commerce, including electronic storefront, on-line business, consumer interface, business-to-business networking, digital payment, legal issues, information product development, and electronic business models. Indispensable for academics and professionals who are interested in Electronic Commerce and Internet Business.

1999. XII, 724 pp. 112 figs., 43 tabs. (International Handbooks on Information Systems)
Hardcover *DM 249 / £ 96 / FF 938 /
Lit. 275.000
ISBN 3-540-65822-X

Please order from · Springer GmbH & Co. Customer Service
Haberstr. 7 · D - 69126 Heidelberg, Germany
Tel.: +49 6221 345 200 · Fax: +49 6221 300 186
e-mail: orders@springer.de
or through your bookseller

Springer

* Recommended retail prices. Prices and other details are subject to change without notice. In EU countries the local VAT is effective. d&p · 66575/4 SF · Gha

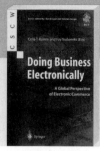

C.T. Romm, F. Sudweeks (Eds.)

Doing Business Electronically

A Global Perspective of Electronic Commerce

Electronic commerce is regarded as one of the most important commercial uses of information technology in recent times. As more and more companies adopt networking technology, ways of doing business are changing dramatically and electronic commerce is proving invaluable for dealing with suppliers, customers and partners distributed across the globe. This volume provides a collection of readings covering all the major areas of electronic commerce, including those related to the World Wide Web. It does not focus on technical issues, but instead examines the general, commercial, social and cultural aspects of using electronic commerce. Invaluable reading material for final year undergraduate and postgraduate students on courses in Electronic Commerce and Computer-Mediated Communication. It will also provide supplementary reading for courses in Business Information Technology, Information Systems, Organisational Change and Project Management.

1st ed. 1998, 2nd printing 1999. XIII, 220 pp. 34 figs. (Computer Supported Cooperative Work)
Softcover *DM 89 / £ 29.50 / FF 336 / Lit. 98.290
ISBN 3-540-76159-4

F. Sudweeks, C.T. Romm (Eds.)

Doing Business on the Internet

Opportunities and Pitfalls

The Internet is currently the fastest-growing and most widely-used technology for doing business electronically. Yet, despite its obvious advantages, it is clear that it is fraught with problems: customers are reluctant to use it for purchasing products; surfing is time-consuming and costly; and users are rapidly becoming disillusioned with its failure to fulfill early promises. In an invaluable follow-up to „Doing Business Electronically", this book provides a collection of readings which look objectively at what Internet commerce can offer both the consumer and the provider. Primarily of interest to researchers and students in areas such as electronic commerce, business strategy, management of information systems, project management and organisational change, it will also be of interest to corporate managers involved with developing their company's Internet-based strategies and to anyone interested in how to buy or sell on the Internet.

1999. VI, 289 pp. 39 figs. (Computer Supported Cooperative Work)
Softcover *DM 99 / £ 35 / FF 373 / Lit. 109.330
ISBN 1-85233-030-9

Please order from · Springer GmbH & Co. Customer Service
Haberstr. 7 · D - 69126 Heidelberg, Germany
Tel.: +49 6221 345 200 · Fax: +49 6221 300 186
e-mail: orders@springer.de
or through your bookseller

* Recommended retail prices. Prices and other details are subject to change without notice. In EU countries the local VAT is effective. d&p · 66575/3 SF · Gha

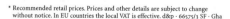

Springer

H.G. Danielmeyer, Y. Takeda (Eds.)

The Company of the Future

Markets, Tools, and Strategies

The art of managing innovative companies
is disclosed in this unique book which
resulted from the first common EU-MITI
project. The Company of the Future will
need new management tools in order to
meet four essential requirements: The first
three are to redirect the attention of management to the internal challenges, to
reveal problems well before final financial
data are available, and to integrate basic
management concepts from all business
functions (marketing, R&D, production,
services, finance, strategy). The fourth
requirement is that tools should be simple
enough to be implemented by busy people
and sufficiently sophisticated to meet the
challenges of the future. This book reveals
those practical, simple and effective tools
for global success and competitiveness.

From the reviews:
*„This is a challenging book about the likely
shape of companies in the 21st century."
(David T. Thompson)*

1999. XX, 208 pp. 64 figs., 23 tabs.
Hardcover *DM 98 / £ 37.50 / FF 370 / Lit. 108.230
ISBN 3-540-65861-0

A. Zerdick, et al.

E-conomics

The Economy of E-Commerce
and the Internet

The finest scientists in communication
economics from the U.S. and Europe have
collaborated to provide an in-depth analysis of the Internet revolution and how the
rules of the game have changed in an economy that trades in information instead of
industrial goods. The book focuses on the
European telecommunications industry,
featuring strategies for a successful Network Economy, as well as an emphasis
on the network infrastructure and the
importance of compatible technological
standards. Essential reading for econo-
mists and business strategists requiring
an understanding of the dynamics of
electronic commerce.

1999. Approx. 345 pp. (European Communication
Council Report, JG 1998/e)
Hardcover *DM 98 / £ 37.50 / FF 370 / Lit. 108.230
ISBN 3-540-64943-3

Please order from · Springer GmbH & Co. Customer Service
Haberstr. 7 · D - 69126 Heidelberg, Germany
Tel.: +49 6221 345 200 · Fax: +49 6221 300 186
e-mail: orders@springer.de
or through your bookseller

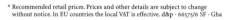

* Recommended retail prices. Prices and other details are subject to change
without notice. In EU countries the local VAT is effective. d&p · 66575/6 SF · Gha

Springer